Twentieth-century dance in Britain

Distributed By
Princeton Book Co. Publishers
P.O. Box 109, Princeton, NJ 08540

TWENTIETH-CENTURY DANCE IN BRITAIN

A history of major dance companies in Britain

Edited by Joan W. White

DANCE BOOKS
9 Cecil Court London WC2

First published in 1985 by Dance Books Ltd., 9 Cecil Court,
London WC2N 4EZ.
ISBN 0 903102 85 4
© 1985 Dance Books Ltd.

Distributed in the USA by Princeton Book Co., P.O. Box 109,
Princeton, N.J. 08540.

British Library Cataloguing in Publication Data

Twentieth-century dance in Britain: a history of
major dance companies in Britain.

1. Ballet -- Great Britain   2. Dance production

I. White, Joan W.

792.8'0941   GV1785.8

Design by Peter Hurst
Design and production in association with
Book Production Consultants, 47 Norfolk Street, Cambridge CB1 2LE
Typeset by Westholme Graphics Ltd.
Printed and bound by The Burlington Press (Cambridge) Ltd,
Foxton, Cambridge

Contents

Illustrations

Acknowledgements

The writers wish to acknowledge with gratitude the many people who, through their co-operation directly and indirectly, have made this publication possible: the directors, administrators and company archivists who have released information and made themselves available to answer questions; photographers Nobby Clark, Colin Clarke, William Cooper, Anthony Crickmay, Zoë Dominic, Antonia Reeve, Frank Sharman and Leslie Spatt who have generously given permission for the text to be illustrated with their work; the B.B.C. Hulton Picture Library and the Theatre Museum who have allowed photographs from their collections to be reproduced; Peter Brinson, Francesca Franchi, Sue Hoyle, Jane Pritchard, John Travis and John Webley, to whom particular thanks are due for giving help and encouragement so patiently and willingly over the past three years. Finally the editor is indebted to David Leonard for his unfailing concern, ready response and meticulous eye for detail.

Joan W. White
October 1983

Preface

History is concerned with changes which take place through time and the subject matter of this book is about changes in dance that have occurred in the twentieth century in Britain, specifically in the development of five major companies, Ballet Rambert, The Royal Ballet and Sadler's Wells Royal ballet, London Festival Ballet, London Contemporary Dance Theatre and The Scottish Ballet. These are not the only major dance companies in Britain but this book arose as a direct response to the development of examinations in school and in particular to the University of London's G.C.E. 'O' level Dance, first examined in June 1983. The repertoires, personalities and policies of these five companies constitute a major area of study in the syllabus. However it is anticipated that the book, written with the young reader in mind, will be of interest and use to all who want to increase their knowledge of the development of dance in Britain.

Fundamental to the study of dance is the need to dance, to choreograph dances, to watch dances, and to learn about the dances themselves, choreographers who created them, designers who designed them, composers who wrote music for them, dancers who danced in them, and the policies which governed their production. It is hoped that this book will encourage young people to focus attention on dances through attending theatre performances and watching dance on film, video and television and in so doing to begin to identify important features of the dance itself and to ask questions about the context in which these dances were choreographed and danced. A book about dance cannot replace the experience of dancing, making dances or watching dances but it can enhance each of these processes by increasing understanding, and this is the aim of this text.

Introduction

In the 1980s there is what is often described as a dance explosion. There are classes available throughout Britain in recreative dance, social dance, ethnic dance and a variety of styles or genres of theatre dance: classical ballet, contemporary dance, tap dance, jazz dance and many others. In the major cities and towns companies both large and small perform regularly, and increasingly dance may be viewed on television. In the early 1900s however the picture was very different. Such theatre dance that existed consisted of items in music hall and opera programmes. A whole evening's performance of dance was unheard of and there was no such thing as modern dance. In the space of just eighty years, then, many changes have occurred.

The dance that existed in music hall programmes consisted of *divertissement* and short ballets often with elaborate stage effects. Often foreign ballerinas were soloists with British dancers as the *corps de ballet*. Two British dancers who made their débuts here and played important roles in the development of ballet in this country are Ninette de Valois and Phyllis Bedells. Significantly Anna Pavlova danced in music halls throughout Britain and when the Diaghilev company first appeared in London in 1911 they did so as part of an opera season.

Such events, however, built an interest in dance and by the mid-1920s British dancers were training more seriously and there was an audience for the art. Nonetheless there were still no British dance companies as such though in 1920 Marie Rambert had formed her Ballet Club and in 1926 Ninette de Valois opened her Academy of Choreographic Art. These two great ladies, both of whom had been associated with Diaghilev's Ballets Russes, were to become extremely significant in the development of dance in Britain. Almost all developments in dance in this country prior to the 1960s and many developments subsequently may be directly attributed to them.

Sadly, Marie Rambert died in 1982 but the company which bears her name, Ballet Rambert, lives on as a constant memorial to her.

Ballet Rambert is the oldest company in existence in Britain and its history is described in the opening chapter.

De Valois' company was formed later than that of Marie Rambert but it grew quickly under her watchful eye and by the early 1950s was both strong and successful, able to mount full-scale classics, fed by a regular stream of talented young dancers from its own school and with a permanent base at the Royal Opera House. It was perhaps logical therefore that this company should become Britain's national ballet. Granted a Royal Charter in 1956, the company took the name The Royal Ballet and the school, The Royal Ballet School. The touring company is now named Sadler's Wells Royal Ballet, acknowledging The Royal Ballet's long-standing association with the Sadler's Wells Theatre. The story of the Royal companies and school is related in chapter 2.

The formation of both Ballet Rambert, originally the Marie Rambert Dancers, and The Royal Ballet, originally the Vic-Wells Ballet, occurred within a few years of the deaths of Diaghilev in 1929 and Anna Pavlova in 1931. Both had helped to prepare the ground for the development of dance in Britain through building audiences who were interested in the art. However their deaths had left a gap not only for audiences in Britain but for the dancers and teachers who had worked in their companies. Many such people were to stay in Britain and to contribute to the development of dance both by performing in the infant Rambert and Vic-Wells companies, reconstructing works from the Diaghilev repertoire, and by teaching. Two British dancers who had danced with Diaghilev's Ballets Russes in its latter days and had subsequently danced in the early Rambert and Vic-Wells companies were Alicia Markova and Anton Dolin and it was they who founded Britain's third major ballet company, London Festival Ballet, in 1951. It is partly due to this heritage that there has always been a strong representation of former Diaghilev works in the company repertoire, as may be seen in chapter 3.

Modern dance, as exhibited in the repertoires of London Contemporary Dance Theatre and Ballet Rambert today, was unknown in Britain until the 1960s. Modern dance forms existed from the 1900s onwards but these were different in style and might best be described as Greek inspired and arising from the influence of Isadora Duncan. Revived Greek Dance, Margaret Morris Movement and Natural Movement, as these major British modern dance forms were called, all found a place in the theatre though significantly none challenged the supremacy of the, by then, fast-growing Ballet Rambert and Sadler's Wells Ballet.

It was to take a shock from the other side of the Atlantic to do this. This shock took the form of an amazing woman, Martha Graham, who almost single handed developed a complete technique of the body, a technique which, it may be argued, is as codified as that of classical ballet. Graham's first visit to Britain was in 1954 but at this time the dance-going public, used as it was to the graceful, harmonious lines of classical ballet, was not ready for Graham's austerity. She played to almost empty houses. Less than a decade later, however, the story was very different, and soon after not only did Britain's oldest company, Ballet Rambert, change from being a classical to a modern company (see chapter 1) but under the directorship of Robin Howard and Robert Cohan a new company, London Contemporary Dance Theatre, was formed. This history of this company is described in chapter 4.

Although today many areas can boast their own dance company, regionally based groups and companies are a comparatively new development. A pioneer in this area was Elizabeth West who with Peter Darrell was convinced of the necessity to take dance outside the capital. With this object in mind Western Theatre Ballet, a forerunner of both The Scottish Ballet and Northern Ballet Theatre, was formed. The story of The Scottish Ballet is taken up in chapter 5.

Within this text the companies are ordered chronologically according to their declared date of origin. In order to help the young student of dance, each chapter describes the formation and development of the company emphasising personalities, policies and achievements. At the end of each chapter is a chart showing, at a glance, significant dates in the company history. There follows a choreochronicle of the dances mentioned in the chapter. This gives details of the title, date, choreographer, composer and designer of the dance, together with details of the first performance if originally performed by another company. Many of the dances mentioned are currently in the respective company repertoires and there is no better way of studying the companies' history than actually going to see the dances that are our heritage. These dances which appear in the choreochronicle are not the only dances in each company repertoire and suggested further reading lists appear at the end of each chapter so that students may follow up areas of enquiry which have been omitted from this text. Finally each chapter ends with a list of questions. It is always useful to know the expectations of examiners. The questions on each company are designed to help dance students prepare for the questions on their examination papers. The appendices include information on who to contact within each company for further help and a glossary of terms used in the text.

However well intentioned, any book can only cover a limited area. The focus of this book is five major dance companies and this is perhaps both a strength and a weakness: a strength since the five major companies described appear within the same cover and with similar emphases, a weakness because as stated earlier there are other companies equally worthy of study and it is to be hoped that these may be the subject of a future book.

History happens all the time, all around us. A company performance today is history tomorrow. The best way of studying history of dance is to go to see the companies perform, read programmes carefully and then try to relate what is seen to what is shown on video, written in newspapers, periodicals and within this and other books.

Chapter 1

Ballet Rambert

Jenny Mann

The history of Ballet Rambert can be divided into three distinct periods as follows:

1926–45	the formation and early years,
1945–66	development into a major classical ballet company,
1966–present day	rebirth as a contemporary dance company.

Ballet Rambert 1926–45:
The formation and early years

The background

Marie Rambert

Ballet Rambert is named after its founder, Marie Rambert, who was born in 1888 in Warsaw, Poland. Marie Rambert took ballet lessons as a girl and always had a passion for dancing, but at first she did not seriously consider dance as a career and her parents sent her to Paris, intending that she should study medicine. While she was a student she saw some performances by the legendary American dancer, Isadora Duncan, which deeply moved her and made her determined to dance herself. She especially admired Duncan's revolutionary freedom of dress and movement and her use of great classical music as the inspiration for her dancing.

Rambert joined a group in Paris led by Isadora's brother, Raymond Duncan, and began to give dance recitals herself which were strongly influenced by Isadora's style. She then studied for three years at the Jaques-Dalcroze school in Dresden, Germany. Dalcroze taught his own system of training called eurhythmics, a method of understanding a piece of music by interpreting the rhythm and melody through physical movement. Because she had become expert in eurythmics, Rambert, at the age of twenty-four, was chosen by Diaghilev in 1912 to join the Ballets Russes and work as assistant to the dancer Vaslav Nijinsky. The Russian composer Igor Stravinsky had written the music and the scenario for a new ballet, *The Rite of Spring*, which Nijinsky was to choreograph. At that time Stravinsky's score was thought to be extremely difficult to dance to as its rhythms are very complicated. Rambert worked with Nijinsky throughout the many arduous rehearsals that he needed to create this ballet. She came to know and understand the great dancer very well, and she was particularly impressed by Nijinsky's determined attempt to extend dance language beyond the conventional ballet steps. For *The Rite of Spring* he invented unusually stylised, often awkward and violent movements to express the primitive and rhythmic music.

Inspired by the example of brilliant Russian dancers such as Nijinsky and Tamara Karsavina, Marie Rambert now began to train seriously in classical ballet for the first time. She danced in the *corps de ballet* of several Ballets Russes productions, including

16

Nijinsky's *L'Après-midi d'un Faune* and *The Rite of Spring*. Through working with the Ballets Russes she came to admire the ballets of the great classical choreographers such as Petipa and Fokine. After Nijinsky left the Ballets Russes Rambert left also. With the outbreak of the First World War she settled in England, making a living by teaching eurhythmics and ballet and giving occasional dance recitals in private homes. She married the distinguished English playwright Ashley Dukes, who was to be an immense source of ideas, advice and support in the years ahead. They had two daughters, Angela and Helena (Lulu), both of whom became dancers and teachers of ballet.

Marie Rambert's enormous fund of energy, her lively mind and even livelier tongue, were the driving forces behind her company throughout its history. Her high spirits used to find expression in her famous cartwheels, which she would turn on every manner of occasion right up until her seventieth birthday, at which point Ashley Dukes forbade her to continue. She possessed to an extraordinary degree the ability to seek out undiscovered talent in others and then to inspire or bully them into proving themselves. Under her influence, Ballet Rambert has provided over the years a constant stream of important new choreographers and dancers to enrich other companies both in Britain and abroad. Rambert took a deep personal interest in her dancers and cultivated their appreciation of all the arts by introducing them to books, poetry, music and painting. She was able to create a very special type of dancer, with an intelligent dramatic quality which has always been apparent in Ballet Rambert productions. In 1962 Marie Rambert was honoured by being made a Dame Commander of the British Empire, in recognition of her life's work for ballet in this country. Until well into her nineties she continued to give enthusiastic support to her company, coming to watch rehearsals and dispensing advice and criticism. She was a vigorous presence at all major events in the British dance world. She died in June 1982, at the age of 94.

It is important to realise that before the 1920s there was no native tradition of ballet in this country and no British ballet company. The visits of Anna Pavlova's company and Diaghilev's Ballets Russes had created a strong interest and stimulated many young people to train as dancers, but in general ballet was still not regarded as a serious art form. Short dance pieces often appeared as items in the programme at the music halls or as interludes during performances of opera, but the public was not yet accustomed to going to the theatre for an entire evening of ballet. The major classics, such as *Swan Lake* or *The Sleeping Beauty*, were then almost unknown in this country.

Enrico Cecchetti

In 1918 Enrico Cecchetti, the great Italian ballet master and inspired teacher of the Ballets Russes, settled in London and opened a school. Most of the important British dancers of the time, as well as many new pupils, went to his studio. They also had the benefit of learning from the example of some of the best Russian dancers who joined the classes whenever the Ballets Russes visited London. Cecchetti's teaching made an immensely valuable impact on the development of dance training in this country and his work was continued afterwards by the many ballet teachers who had studied with him. Marie Rambert continued to train with him until he left England in 1923 and he had a profound influence on her own teaching of classical ballet.

The Rambert School of Ballet

In 1920 Marie Rambert collected her pupils together and opened her own ballet school in West London. This eventually grew into the Rambert School of Ballet, but at first it was simply a rented studio in which she gave her classes: the dancers practised mostly in cold, damp and draughty church halls. Nevertheless from the beginning Rambert had some outstandingly gifted pupils and she was able to mould them into dancers of great talent. Among her earliest students was Diana Gould, who so impressed Diaghilev that he invited her to join the Ballets Russes. By the mid-1920s an exceptional group of students had been assembled, including Andrée Howard, who later mader her name as a choreographer, Maude Lloyd, Pearl Argyle, William Chappell, a talented designer as well as a dancer, Harold Turner, who became the first British virtuoso male dancer, and Frederick Ashton.

The birth of Ballet Rambert

The year 1926 is a significant one in the history of Ballet Rambert. It marks the first ever public performances given by Rambert's group of students, who were called the Marie Rambert Dancers for the occasion, but who later became known as Ballet Rambert. The company therefore dates its birth from these performances. The event was a mixed revue called *Riverside Nights* which took place at the Lyric Theatre in Hammersmith. The Marie Rambert Dancers were asked to contribute an item to this revue, and the ballet they performed was *A Tragedy of Fashion*. This is also significant for being the first choreography by Frederick Ashton.

Frederick Ashton

Frederick Ashton spent his childhood in South America, where he was deeply impressed by seeing Anna Pavlova dance. He arrived at Marie Rambert's studio in 1924, sent by Massine, from whom he had been taking ballet lessons. His avowed ambition was to be a great dancer like Nijinsky, but although he did become an important dancer in Rambert's company his major contribution was as a choreographer.

Marie Rambert, the founder of Ballet Rambert, and Frederick Ashton dancing the lead roles in Ashton's first ballet, A Tragedy of Fashion, *1926. This was also the first public performance by Ballet Rambert. The designs are by Sophie Fedorovitch.*
Photo: Betram Park.

Marie Rambert, on seeing Ashton improvise some steps in the studio, decided that he might have choreographic talent and pushed him into making his first ballet. The theme for *A Tragedy of Fashion* was adapted from a suggestion by Ashley Dukes. It was a satirical piece about a fashion designer who is driven to despair by the failure of his latest creation and stabs himself to death with a large pair of scarlet scissors. Ashton danced the role of the designer, partnered by Marie Rambert as his assistant. *A Tragedy of Fashion* was quite a success and Diaghilev went to see it more than once and was highly complimentary. This encouraged Ashton to continue to experiment with choreography. Over the next few years the Marie Rambert Dancers put on occasional performances and Ashton made several more short ballets for them, including *Capriol Suite* in 1930.

In the early 1930s Ashton became the main contributor to the repertory of Rambert's company. For the Ballet Club between 1931 and 1935 he choreographed no less than eleven new ballets, including *La Péri*, *Foyer de Danse*, *Les Masques* and *Mephisto Valse*. In these last four works the leading roles were created by Alicia Markova, an English dancer who had been a ballerina with the Ballets Russes before that company had broken up in 1929. In these early ballets Ashton laid the foundations for his own characteristic style: elegant and witty, and with a concern for purely classical dancing. In 1935 Ashton left to join the Vic-Wells Ballet as principal choreographer. He had outgrown Marie Rambert's small company and needed the more secure position and greater opportunities that the larger, wealthier organisation could offer him.

The Mercury Theatre
In 1927 Ashley Dukes bought a church hall in Notting Hill Gate, West London, and converted it into a studio for his wife's rapidly expanding ballet school and a theatre, which they called the Mercury Theatre. It had a small stage, no more than eighteen feet square, and it could hold an audience of 150. There was a staircase running down on to the back of the stage which Ashton incorporated into the choreography of several of his productions. This tiny theatre has been called the cradle of British ballet, because many of the greatest dancers and choreographers this country has known have tried out their first steps on its stage. The Mercury was the home base of Ballet Rambert until the mid-1960s and part of the Rambert School of Ballet remains there still.

The Ballet Club period, 1930–39

The Ballet Club

The Ballet Club was another idea from Ashley Dukes. It was formed in 1930 and performances started early in 1931 at the Mercury Theatre, continuing until the onset of the Second World War in 1939. The aim of the Ballet Club was to promote the art of ballet by forming a society of supporters, including people who were influential in English social life and the arts, and by offering them regular performances in a cultured atmosphere. It was also intended to foster new creative talent among British chor-eographers, composers and designers, by providing them with the opportunity to experiment and to show their work to a select and appreciative audience.

Ballet Club performances took place mainly on Sunday even-ings. This was because Marie Rambert had hardly any money with which to pay her dancers. They had to support themselves by appearing elsewhere and so were normally only available on Sundays. Occasionally it was possible to arrange a mid-week performance. Rambert would pay them a few shillings each which would barely cover their expenses, and they were expected to buy their own ballet shoes, a costly item. Nevertheless her dancers lived for these performances and willingly gave up their Sundays in order to have the chance to participate in them. They were all infected with Rambert's spirit of enthusiasm for creating ballet in this country and there was always a feeling of intense excitement in the air at Ballet Club rehearsals.

As well as the regular performances at the Ballet Club, from the mid-1930s the company began to present longer summer seasons at the Mercury. In 1934 it gave its first West End season, at the Duke of York's Theatre in London. During 1935 the title Ballet Rambert was adopted and the company has borne this name ever since. During the 1930s Ballet Rambert and the Ballet Club played a vital part in developing new British talent. Important dancers to emerge at this time included Elisabeth Schooling, Peggy van Praagh, who later became Director of the Australian Ballet, Hugh Laing, Walter Gore and Frank Staff. The last two also later became notable choreographers.

It was of the utmost importance to Marie Rambert that the British ballet tradition which was now developing, under the guidance of Ballet Rambert and the Vic-Wells Ballet, should be firmly based on the best of the classical heritage. She was particularly concerned with continuing the exciting innovations of the Ballets Russes with which she herself had been closely involved. Following the deaths of Diaghilev in 1929 and Anna Pavlova in 1931 both of their companies broke up. The serious loss to the West of these two influential Russian companies had a fortunate outcome for British ballet: many of the Russian-trained dancers settled in this country and so were able to hand on their expertise to the new generation of dancers here.

Tamara Karsavina

The first to arrive was Tamara Karsavina, who was prima ballerina of the Ballets Russes. She generously agreed to appear as a guest artist when the Marie Rambert Dancers presented their first extended seasons, which took place at the Lyric Theatre, Hammersmith during summer and Christmas time 1930. Karsavina undertook to teach Fokine's *Les Sylphides* to Rambert's dancers and performed the leading role, which she had originally created in 1905. As she had learned the ballet directly from Fokine, Karsavina could communicate not merely the correct steps but the whole meaning of the work. It was of necessity a small-scale production, owing to the limited finances and number of dancers available, but it was judged very successful in capturing the romantic mood of the earlier version. Karsavina also appeared in Fokine's *Le Spectre de la Rose* and *Le Carnaval*, again recreating her original leading roles in these ballets. Her dancing was an enormous inspiration to Marie Rambert's fledgeling company.

Alicia Markova

Another star ballerina of the Ballets Russes, Alicia Markova, found a home at the Ballet Club for several years in the early 1930s. She performed in extracts from *Swan Lake* and *The Sleeping Beauty* and took over the main part in *Les Sylphides* from Karsavina. She also created roles in many of Ashton's new ballets at that time.

Leon Woizikowski, an outstanding character dancer from the Ballets Russes, was a guest artist at the Ballet Club for a period. He produced *L'Après-midi d'un Faune*, which he had learned directly from Nijinsky, and also Fokine's *Le Carnaval*. Another most welcome visitor was Kyra Nijinsky, the daughter of Vaslav, who appeared briefly with the Ballet Club while she was in London. A very expressive dancer with the same strong dramatic presence as her father, she added extra life to those performances in which she took part.

Antony Tudor

Antony Tudor was another major British choreographer to emerge from Marie Rambert's studio during the Ballet Club period. He started coming to classes in 1929, turning up at four in the afternoon after working from five in the morning as an accountant at Smithfield meat market. Suitably impressed by this dedication, Rambert gave him a job as her secretary and stage manager so that he could devote his time entirely to ballet. Tudor began to choreograph two years later and went on to contribute several very

Members of the original cast of Antony Tudor's Dark Elegies, 1937. *From left to right: Antony Tudor, Maude Lloyd, Peggy van Praagh, Agnes de Mille and Walter Gore.*
Photo: Houston Rogers. The Theatre Museum Crown Copyright.

important works to the Ballet Club repertory. These included *The Planets* and *Jardin aux Lilas (Lilac Garden)*. He also made some ballets especially for television, at that time a newly developing medium but one which was quickly recognised as having great potential for dance. In 1937 he made *Dark Elegies*, a deeply moving work about parents grieving for their lost children who have been killed in a terrible disaster. *Dark Elegies* was seen to mark a new phase in British ballet because it showed how dance could be used to portray strong human emotions. It was also influential for its combination of classical movement with very modern choreography.

In 1937 Tudor left the Ballet Club to form his own company. At the beginning of the war this company was disbanded and Ballet Rambert took over some of its repertory, including Tudor's *Judgement of Paris*, a satire on the famous Greek legend in which the three goddesses are seen as tired prostitutes in a seedy café. In 1939 Tudor accepted an invitation to go to the United States of America to join the newly formed American Ballet Theatre and since then his reputation as a choreographer has been largely made in that country. Ballet Rambert has continued to present his early works: indeed, *Dark Elegies* and *Judgement of Paris* are the only ballets from the company's classical period to remain in its modern repertory.

Andrée Howard

Several other talented young choreographers created work for the Ballet Club. Foremost was Andrée Howard, who had been one of the Marie Rambert Dancers. She made more than a dozen ballets for the company over the years. Among her successes were *Cinderella, Death and the Maiden* and *The Sailor's Return*. One of her most memorable was *Lady into Fox*, based on the novel by David Garnett. This is about a young wife who turns into a fox and escapes from her home into the forest. The leading part was taken by Sally Gilmour, who proved herself to be a very fine dancer-actress and who went on to create many more important roles. Howard, together with Susan Salaman, also choreographed *Mermaid*, based on the Hans Anderson fairy tale of the little mermaid. Susan Salaman is best known for her series of very clever and witty ballets called *Sporting Sketches* which parodied various English sports: *Le Rugby, Le Cricket* and *Le Boxing*.

Frank Staff

Another dancer, Frank Staff, also began to choreograph while he was with Ballet Rambert. His works include *Czernyana*, a suite of dances which made fun of the ballet conventions of the day, and *Peter and the Wolf*.

There was a very good relationship between Ballet Rambert and the Vic-Wells Ballet and many of Marie Rambert's dancers who had joined the Vic-Wells continued to perform at the Ballet Club in their free evenings. Margot Fonteyn, Robert Helpmann and Anton Dolin, all principal dancers with the Vic-Wells, also made guest appearances at the Ballet Club from time to time. Ninette de Valois, the founder of the Vic-Wells, was invited by Marie Rambert to choreograph for her dancers, and in 1934 she made *Bar aux Folies-Bergère*, based on a famous painting by Manet.

The Ballet Club introduced a wide range of music into its repertory. Rambert's studies with Dalcroze had given her a deep love and understanding of music which she communicated to her company. She encouraged her choreographers to broaden their musical interest, often suggesting composers and pieces of music that they might use, and so far as was possible the Ballet Club gave opportunities to modern composers to create music for the performances. This was limited by the lack of money available. Most of the accompaniment to the ballets was played on two pianos, although occasionally other solo instruments, such as a violin, were brought in. When the sound of an orchestra was required the music would be played on a gramophone. Only very rarely could a small chamber orchestra be used.

Marie Rambert believed strongly in design as being a vitally important element in the creation of a ballet. In this she was following the example set by Diaghilev, who revolutionised ballet design with the Ballets Russes. As there was hardly any money for costumes and sets, Ballet Club designers had to rely on imagination and inventiveness rather than on lavish materials to produce their effects. Several of the dancers also developed talents as designers, including Andrée Howard, William Chappell and Hugh Laing.

Sophie Fedorovtch

The most important designer that Marie Rambert discovered at this time was Sophie Fedorovitch. She designed Ashton's first ballet, *A Tragedy of Fashion*, and this was the start of a long and close working relationship between herself and Ashton which set a high standard for ballet design over the years. Fedorovitch worked closely with the choreographer and composer to create the right mood for each ballet, and her designs had a strong simplicity of line and colour which was very effective dramatically. Her work has been a major influence on ballet design in Britain.

The war years, 1939–45

The Second World War presented immense difficulties for the continuation of Ballet Rambert. Evening performances were banned because of the blitz, many London theatres closed down, and the Ballet Club had to be ended. Most of the male dancers were called up, although they were sometimes able to appear with the company when they were on leave. Then the Arts Theatre in the West End began a series of lunchtime performances which proved extremely popular. Workers would arrive from their various duties and eat their sandwiches during the show. This success was followed up with afternoon and teatime ballet, until the dancers found themselves giving several performances a day in different theatres. Later on, the Council for the Encouragement of Music and the Arts (C.E.M.A.), took on the management of Ballet Rambert to help in the war effort and contribute to raising public morale by providing entertainment for the workers and armed forces. Ballet Rambert accordingly toured all around Britain, appearing in factory canteens, hostels and army camps. This often meant performing under very difficult conditions, with tiny stages, uneven flooring and few backstage facilities. Here the dancers' experience gained from the cramped space at the Mercury Theatre was very helpful.

The activities of both Ballet Rambert and the Vic-Wells Ballet during the war did have a very beneficial effect for ballet in the future. The widespread performances, often happening in people's own workplaces, were extraordinarily popular and were responsible for introducing many people to ballet who might otherwise never have had the opportunity of seeing it. By the end of the war the audiences had been greatly increased and the following years saw an upsurge in ballet activity.

Ballet Rambert 1945–66, development into a major classical ballet company

Following the end of the war the Arts Council of Great Britain continued to support Ballet Rambert and began to give the company a small annual grant, which increased gradually over the years. This money enabled the company to enlarge itself to some thirty-six dancers, and the new intake included the very young but highly talented Belinda Wright and John Gilpin. Sally Gilmour had become the principal dancer. From now on an orchestra was employed on a regular basis to accompany the performances.

In 1946 Ballet Rambert gave its first season at Sadler's Wells Theatre in Islington. This was the home of the Sadler's Wells Ballet. The summer season at Sadler's Wells became an annual event, and the fact that the company could now fill this large theatre, which holds an audience of about 1,500, was proof of its growth in popularity. Seasons were also given at the King's Theatre in Hammersmith. By now Ballet Rambert had completely outgrown the tiny Mercury Theatre and required a larger stage to mount its productions and a bigger house for its audiences. The Mercury continued to be used as the base for company rehearsals and the Rambert School, so the close contact between Ballet Rambert and the school which supplied it with many of its new dancers was maintained. However over the next twenty years the company suffered badly from not having a London theatre of its own to use as a home base in which to choreograph and perform.

Classical productions

The major achievement of Ballet Rambert during this time was the remounting of a series of ballets from the classical period. Indeed Ballet Rambert built a reputation for its small-scale but beautifully produced versions of the classical, and especially romantic ballets, all of which showed Marie Rambert's dedication to recreating the detail and spirit of the original choreography. These ballets had inevitably to be produced on a very limited budget and were triumphs for Rambert's method of achieving the highest possible artistic standards on very slender means. The great post-war success was the mounting of the company's first full-length ballet, *Giselle*, in 1946. In order to understand fully the feeling and meaning behind each movement, Rambert sought out the poems of

Heinrich Heine which were the original inspiration for the choreography. The poems tell the German legend of the Wilis,
'maidens who have died before their wedding day, because of
faithless lovers', who return at night to take their revenge on men.
By paying this attention to the sources of the ballet, Rambert was
able to recapture the romantic atmosphere it embodied. The production was very highly praised and had a great influence on later
revivals by other companies in this country. Sally Gilmour was a
fragile and moving Giselle, with Walter Gore as her partner,
Albrecht. It was over ten years before Ballet Rambert could follow
up this success with more full-length classical productions.

In 1957 the company mounted *Coppélia*, which became by far its
greatest popular attraction during this period. In 1960 Marie

---

An example of Ballet Rambert's classical period: Act Two of Swan Lake, *from
the 1940s. The principal dancers are Sally Gilmour as Odette and Walter Gore
as Prince Siegfried (standing).*
Photo: Frank H. Sharman.

Rambert was able to stage a second ballet from the romantic era, *La Sylphide*. This was produced by Elsa Marianne von Rosen, who came specially from Denmark to teach the Bournonville style of movement to the dancers. This was the first British production of the Bournonville version of this ballet. In 1962 Ballet Rambert achieved the first production in the West of the complete *Don Quixote*, which was recreated for the company by the Polish ballet director Witold Borkowski. A new version of *Giselle* was made in 1965. In these later revivals the principal roles were danced by Lucette Aldous. The company continued to perform *Les Sylphides*, as well as extracts from the larger classics *Swan Lake* and *The Nutcracker*, so its classical repertory became considerable. These productions were of an exceptional standard but apart from *Coppélia* they were not always so successful in drawing large audiences. By the 1950s the British public was demanding large-scale and spectacular productions of the familiar and well-loved classics such as *Swan Lake* and *The Sleeping Beauty*. Audiences were less willing to come to see ballets whose titles were then unknown to them, such as *La Sylphide* and *Don Quixote*, and even more unwilling to see new works by modern choreographers.

New choreography

Walter Gore

A considerable number of new works were created over this time, however. In the 1940s Walter Gore emerged as Rambert's principal choreographer. He is especially remembered for *Mr. Punch* in which he danced the central character. Andrée Howard made possibly her finest ballet for the company, *The Sailor's Return*. This was about the wedding of a black girl with an English sailor and the persecution she suffers when he brings her back to his home village. Sally Gilmour danced the part of Tulip, the black girl, and Walter Gore was the sailor. *The Sailor's Return* was the first full-length ballet by an English choreographer. After Gore left in 1950 Marie Rambert found herself for the first time without a major choreographer in her own company. Over the next few years she took into her repertory new ballets by outside choreographers, including *Laiderette* by Kenneth MacMillan and early works by the then relatively unknown John Cranko and Robert Joffrey. It was not until Norman Morrice began to create work in the late 1950s that Ballet Rambert was once again producing choreography of great strength from within its own ranks.

The Ballet Workshop

As Ballet Rambert became increasingly committed to lengthy touring there was less opportunity within the company for discovering and nurturing new choreographic talent. Between 1951 and 1955 the independent Ballet Workshop provided a venue where choreographers could experiment. This was run at the Mercury Theatre by Marie Rambert's daughter, Angela, with her husband David Ellis. Regular performances were given on Sunday evenings, always to packed audiences, and dancers from the established ballet companies were keen to appear. During the four years that it ran, the Ballet Workship presented works by forty choreographers, including Kenneth MacMillan, John Cranko and Peter Darrell, and it also gave commissions to many new composers and designers. By 1955 the Ballet Workshop had itself outgrown the Mercury, and at this time David Ellis decided to join Ballet Rambert and take on the much-needed task of managing and fund-raising for the company. The Ballet Workshop was closed down and David Ellis became Ballet Rambert's Associate Director, where he gave much valuable help over the next ten years, seeing the company through times which were becoming increasingly difficult financially.

Touring

The company's greatest adventure soon after the war was a major tour to Australia and New Zealand in 1947–48. They had been invited for six months but the tour was so successful that it was extended to eighteen months. Despite the great artistic success, this tour had disastrous consequences. Ballet Rambert arrived back in England almost bankrupt. They had brought no money back from Australia and had lost a large number of dancers who had decided to stay behind in Australia, including Sally Gilmour. On their return to England Belinda Wright and John Gilpin also left to join other companies. To complete the disaster, most of the scenery and costumes had been damaged beyond repair during the journey home.

In 1949, with the help of a £500 grant from the Arts Council, Ballet Rambert was able to start again. However it took the company many years to recover and it was ten years before it regained the size and status it had enjoyed before leaving for Australia. Meanwhile it had to undertake as much touring as possible, both in Britain and abroad, in order to survive financially. Over this period it visited France, Belgium, Germany, Italy, Spain,

China, the United States, Greece and the Near East as well as touring extensively in Britain and making regular appearances at the Lyric and King's Theatres and at Sadler's Wells. Paula Hinton at first replaced Sally Gilmour as principal dancer and when she left in 1950 she was succeeded by Lucette Aldous.

The endless touring began to have a serious effect and the 1950s were hard years for Ballet Rambert. Audiences now mainly wanted the classics and so theatre managers in the provinces demanded that the company should provide such performances. But the cost of mounting big classical productions was a severe financial strain. It meant that it was necessary to tour with a *corps de ballet* and a large orchestra and this was very expensive in terms of salaries and travel costs. Touring conditions at this time were very harsh. The company would set out for many weeks at a time, travelling by train on Sundays to the next theatre ready to begin again on Monday morning. The dancers would have to stay in the cheapest lodgings in each town so life was very uncomfortable. Rambert was unable to pay her dancers very much, and their salaries were low compared with those of other ballet companies. A spirit of loyalty held the company together but many dancers found the pressure too great and so left. It had become a constantly repeated pattern by now that Marie Rambert would find and develop new talent and then lose it to other richer ballet companies. Artistically Ballet Rambert was now facing increasing competition from the larger British companies, the Sadler's Wells Ballet and the newly formed London Festival Ballet. Unlike Ballet Rambert, both of these were able to stage the large-scale classics which the provincial audiences wanted. The lack of a London theatre base and time to work in one place were serious handicaps to the creation of new work. Rehearsal periods were largely taken up with teaching the existing repertory to new dancers rather than with making new ballets.

By the 1960s various schemes were being proposed to help Ballet Rambert out of a situation which was becoming increasingly frustrating and depressing, both artistically and financially. For many years it had been intended that the company should raise the money to build a theatre of its own in London. One idea was that Ballet Rambert might share a new theatre with the Royal Shakespeare Company, a plan which came to nothing after the RSC was offered a custom-built theatre of its own at the Barbican. Another scheme which was seriously discussed was the possibility of merging with London Festival Ballet. In the event none of these plans came about. Instead in the mid-sixties a far more radical change took place in the Ballet Rambert company and the person who played a large part in this was Norman Morrice.

Norman Morrice

Norman Morrice trained at the Rambert School and in 1953 joined the company as a dancer. He had always wanted to choreograph and in 1958 Rambert gave him his chance. He made *Two Brothers*, a modern dance-drama about jealousy between two brothers which results in one killing the other. The brothers were danced by Morrice and John Chesworth, both of whom later became artistic directors for the company. Morrice was always interested in making ballets on modern themes with realistic characters, and he built up a following among younger members of the audiences. He was appointed associate choreographer and continued to produce one new ballet every year, which was all the time for creative work that could be spared. The continuation of his story takes us into Ballet Rambert's modern period.

Ballet Rambert 1966 – the present day, rebirth as a contemporary dance company

Norman Morrice

In the early1960's Norman Morrice visited the United States of America to study the developments in modern dance there. He greatly admired the achievements of Martha Graham in forging her own dance technique and in pioneering a new style of dance production and he was also impressed by the work of other American choreographers such as Glen Tetley, Merce Cunningham and Anna Sokolow. Morrice returned to Britain convinced that this was the direction in which Ballet Rambert should be moving. In 1966 Morrice came to Marie Rambert and outlined his own plan for the future. In essence this was as follows: to dismiss the *corps de ballet* and streamline the company to less than twenty dancers, all of soloist standard; to reduce the size of the orchestra; to introduce contemporary dance training, basically that of Martha Graham, for the remaining dancers; and to create a new repertory of contemporary work from new choreographers combined with the best of the work from the company's past. In this way Ballet Rambert would become an exciting and innovative dance company once again. Morrice was also inspired by the example of the Dutch company, Nederlands Dans Theater, which had recently successfully undergone a similar change in artistic policy.

Marie Rambert, by now seventy-eight years old, seized on this idea of making a revoluntionary change in her company with all her usual enthusiasm. She insisted on appointing Morrice to be her associate director and she gave him her wholehearted support. The change went ahead and on 2 July 1966 the old-style Ballet Rambert gave its last performance. By 18th July it had been transformed and the new Ballet Rambert gave its first performance in November. As Marie Rambert, with increasing age, began to withdraw from the day-to-day running of her company Norman Morrice took on more responsibilities and was made co-director. He continued to choregraph when his other duties allowed him the time and gave Ballet Rambert a dozen more new ballets including *Blind Sight, That is the Show* and *Smiling Immortal*. In 1974 Morrice left to become a free-lance choreographer and he was later appointed artistic director of The Royal Ballet.

Policies of the new Ballet Rambert

In the 1960s in this country classical ballet and Graham-based contemporary dance were still largely perceived as being completely separate and opposed. But Rambert and Morrice had the foresight to see that it would be possible to create a company which is founded on a fusion of the two techniques and which performs choreography combining the best elements of both. The policy was then, and remains today, to train the dancers in both classical ballet and contemporary dance, thus developing broadly based and versatile performers who are ready to work in a wide range of dance styles. Ballet Rambert now returned to the ideals of the Ballet Club days, of being a truly creative company, pioneering new styles in choreography, music and design and encouraging new choreographers to emerge from within the company. The feeling of excitement which had been lacking for far too many years was rekindled.

One element in Morrice's original policy proved to be unworkable in practice. At first the intention had been to revive the most interesting of the ballets from the company's early years, especially works by Ashton, Tudor, Howard and Gore. For a couple of years this did begin to happen, but it was found that the old ballets looked very dated alongside the contemporary work and the two styles did not fit well together. So regretfully it was decided to drop most of the older ballets, with the exception of some of Tudor's. Most of Ballet Rambert's early repertory is now never seen on stage.

Rebuilding the company

It took four months in 1966 to reorganise and rehearse the new company and this was made possible by a continued grant from the Arts Council, which gave its full support to the bold changes that were being made. Meanwhile, David Ellis had resigned as associate director, and he and his wife Angela Ellis took over the Rambert School of Ballet at the Mercury Theatre. Ballet Rambert moved out and the close relationship between the company and its school which had existed throughout its history was now ended. The company moved into a church hall in Acton, where conditions were much the same as in the early days, and the dancers were once again rehearsing in the damp and cold with few facilities. However in 1971 a generous grant from the Calouste Gulbenkian

Foundation enabled Ballet Rambert to move into a converted furniture warehouse in Chiswick, West London, which is its present home. The building is large enough to provide two dance studios and offices for the administration and publicity departments, as well as space for the wardrobe and the carpentry workshop where the sets are made. Ballet Rambert was under one roof once again.

The major task now facing Norman Morrice was to rebuild an audience for the new Ballet Rambert and this took several years to achieve. Apart from a few visits by American companies such as those of Martha Graham and Merce Cunningham there had been little opportunity to see contemporary dance in this country, especially outside London. There was a prejudice against modern dance among the ballet-going public, who were largely disappointed that Ballet Rambert was no longer performing *Coppélia*. Many dance critics expressed reservations about the new artistic policies and the new ballets did not always meet with critical success. Nevertheless there were people among both critics and public who were greatly interested and excited by the direction the company was taking. The shock of the change stimulated a large volume of mail from audiences, some abusive and some highly enthusiastic. It was found that the response grew far more favourable on a second or third visit to the same theatre, as the new audience began to develop, and this helped to quieten the fears of theatre managers around the country.

Morrice quickly found that the new-style Ballet Rambert had a strong appeal to young people and he therefore worked hard at building up this section of the audience. He started a programme of talks, master classes and demonstrations in colleges, art schools and theatres to explain contemporary dance to young people. The first children's programme, *Bertram Batell's Sideshow*, Bertram Batell being an anagram of Ballet Rambert, was produced in 1970. This show was choreographed jointly by the whole company and was great fun and very popular.

Rambert Dance Unit

Another idea was the Rambert Dance Unit, which was set up in 1972. The Unit, which had four dancers, travelled round the country, teaching and performing in colleges, halls and small theatres which the main company could not reach. The Dance Unit often went ahead to prepare audiences in towns where Ballet Rambert was due to appear. Unfortunately the Unit proved so successful that it made increasing demands in terms of money and organisation, so after twelve months it had to be closed.

Four or five years on from 1966, Ballet Rambert had become a well-integrated company, consisting by now mainly of new dancers. Since the close links with the school had been severed, dancers were now being taken in from widely varying backgrounds and often from foreign dance companies. Morrice was able to mould this diverse talent into a strong group of committed individuals, working in a creative atmosphere and already developing new choreographers within the ranks. Notable members at this time were Lenny Westerdijk, Sandra Craig, Julia Blaikie, Jonathan Taylor, Joseph Scoglio and Christopher Bruce. The company still has no theatre of its own in London. For several years the Jeanetta Cochrane Theatre, a smallish building seating about 350 people, provided a home. By 1973 Ballet Rambert was sufficiently well established to present its first season as a contemporary company at Sadler's Wells Theatre, eight years since it had last performed there. Since then it has continued to use Sadler's Wells for its main London seasons, while still on occasion performing elsewhere in London, such as at the Young Vic and the Roundhouse, both of which theatres attract a predominantly young audience.

Glen Tetley

A major influence in establishing the new Ballet Rambert was the American choreographer Glen Tetley. Tetley was invited by Morrice in 1967 to help in the creation of a new repertory for the company. Tetley had studied medicine before becoming a dancer. He had performed with the Martha Graham Company and then formed his own company, for whom he choreographed his first important work, *Pierrot Lunaire*. This was hailed as a masterpiece and since then Tetley has gained recognition as a leading international choreographer. His work combines classical and contemporary dance to great theatrical effect, and was ideally suited to the artistic policies of the new Ballet Rambert.

Tetley was an enormous help to the dancers in giving them an understanding of the contemporary exercises in which they were

---

Christopher Bruce as Pierrot and Lucy Burge as Columbine in Glen Tetley's Pierrot Lunaire, *recreated for Ballet Rambert in 1967. This ballet made a great impact and played an important part in establishing Ballet Rambert as a modern dance company. It also made Bruce's reputation as a dancer. Photo: Anthony Crickmay.*

now being trained. In 1967 he gave the company four ballets: three recreations, *Pierrot Lunaire, Ricercare* and *Freefall,* and a new work made specially for the Rambert dancers, *Ziggurat.* Tetley continued his close association with Ballet Rambert for many years, returning several times to create new ballets, including *Embrace Tiger and Return to Mountain,* which is based on Chinese Tai-chi movements, *Rag Dances* and *Praeludium.* In 1979 Tetley choreographed a full-length production of *The Tempest,* based on the play by William Shakespeare, with spectacular designs by Nadine Baylis and a specially commissioned musical score by the Norwegian composer Arne Nordheim. *The Tempest* has been an immense success with audiences throughout the country and abroad.

Ballet Rambert established as a creative force in modern dance

At first the repertory showed a strongly American influence, for as well as Tetley, Morrice brought in other guest choreographers from the United States, including Anna Sokolow, Louis Falco and Lar Lubovitch. Morrice hoped that a British tradition of contemporary dance would develop from these influences, and within a short time Rambert members were beginning to produce works of their own. This process was encouraged by giving special workshop performances in which everyone was invited to try their hand. Collaborative seasons were initiated with the Central School of Art and Design, whose students worked with the dancers and provided the designs for the new ballets. These workshop programmes were called *Collaborations I and II.* Morrice also organised two seasons called *Dance for New Dimensions* which took place at the Young Vic Theatre. Here the audience was seated around three sides of the stage, in close contact with the dancers, instead of facing a conventional proscenium arch stage. This presented the young choreographers with the challenge of creating dance suitable for thrust stages, which the company was increasingly meeting in the newer theatres on tour. A large number of dancers choreographed for these workshop seasons, including Jonathan Taylor, who later became artistic director of Australian Dance Theatre, Gideon Avrahami, who founded EMMA Dance Company in the East Midlands, Leigh Warren, John Chesworth and Christopher Bruce.

Christopher Bruce

Within a few years the new Ballet Rambert produced a major

choreographer of its own. This was Christopher Bruce, and together with Tetley he had a strong influence on shaping the style of the company throughout the 1970s. Bruce had trained at the Rambert School and he entered the company towards the end of its classical period. In 1967 Bruce made his reputation as a dancer in Tetley's *Pierrot Lunaire*, in which he gave an outstanding performance as the pathetic-comic Pierrot. He soon became recognised as one of this country's most gifted male dancers, displaying a great dramatic power. At the same time he was developing his talents as a choreographer, making his first ballet, *George Frideric*, in 1969. Since then he has established himself as a leading international choreographer.

Bruce continues the modern Rambert tradition of blending classical and contemporary dance styles, often also including steps from jazz and folk dance to suit the particular mood of each ballet. His choreography is always powerfully emotional and dramatic, qualities which are further brought out through the music and design. Bruce often deals with social or political themes, as in *'for these who die as cattle'*, which comments on the futility of war, *Cruel Garden*, a surreal dance-drama created in collaboration with the mime Lindsay Kemp, which is about the Spanish poet García Lorca who was assassinated during the Spanish Civil War, *Ghost Dances*, which is concerned with the political oppression and suffering of the people of South America, and *Requiem*, a savage attack on the decadent Berlin society of the 1920s which resulted in the holocaust of the Second World War. Despite their serious themes these ballets often contain moments of high comedy and touching insights into human relationships.

Some Bruce ballets use disturbing psychological images, such as those in *Ancient Voices of Children* and *Black Angels*, which he choreographed to startling and aggressive modern music by George Crumb. The effect of both these productions is enhanced by the striking designs of Nadine Baylis. Bruce also makes gentler, sometimes humorous works, such as *Girl with Straw Hat*, a tribute to Marie Rambert on the fiftieth birthday of her company, *Preludes and Song*, about his sadness at seeing his own children grow up too quickly, and *Night with Waning Moon*, which shows the comical antics of Pierrot, Columbine and Harlequin, traditional characters from the Commedia dell'Arte.

Bruce was the associate director for Ballet Rambert from 1975 until 1979, when he resigned to pursue his career as a free-lance choreographer. He remains attached to the company as associate

Christopher Bruce's Ghost Dances, *1981. Dancers from left to right: Hugh Craig, Michael Ho, Yair Vardi.*
Photo: Nobby Clark.

choreographer. His full-length ballet *Cruel Garden*, in which he dances the leading role of the poet, was filmed by BBC television and shown in 1982, and *Ghost Dances* was televised in 1983.

Ballet Rambert's change of artistic policy in 1966 was accompanied by a revolution in its design. Here a strong influence has been the Martha Graham Company, for whom the sculptor Noguchi created powerfully emotive settings for Graham's choreography.

Designers

A major impact on ballet design in this country has been the work of Nadine Baylis, who has created designs for many Rambert ballets, particularly those by Morrice, Tetley and Bruce. Baylis acknowledges Sophie Fedorovitch as the original source of inspiration for her work. She keeps in close contact with the choreographer, dancers and lighting designer during the whole creative process. Her designs use abstract, sculptural shapes, great stretches of material and expansive surfaces to make an exciting environment for the choreography. Important Baylis designs have been for Tetley's *Ziggurat*, a multimedia production in which she used slide projections and clothed the dancers in bizarre net-like body stockings, and her magnificently spectacular creations for

Tetley's *The Tempest*, in which she swathed the stage in coloured silk to represent the sea. For Bruce's *Black Angels* Baylis made a terrifying web-like structure which towered over the dancers, who were clothed in rags torn to ressemble bat's wings. Another important theatre designer who has worked with Ballet Rambert is Ralph Koltai, whose early work included several Morrice ballets such as *Two Brothers*. More recently he made the heavy wooden bullring set for Bruce's *Cruel Garden*. A designer now coming to the fore is Pamela Marre. For Bruce's *Requiem* Marre designed a brilliantly coloured neon-lit nightclub bar. During the second half of the ballet the darkened dismantled shapes of the set become the empty shells of buildings destroyed by war.

A vital aspect of contemporary dance is the exciting contribution made by lighting designers such as John B. Read. Read redesigned Ballet Rambert's lighting system after 1966, and his bold new ideas included the use of side lighting to create startling shadows on the dancers' bodies and give a more sculptural effect. Modern ballets often have little scenery. The reasons for this are partly financial, since it is difficult and expensive to transport large sets around on tour. But many modern choreographers prefer the spectacular and subtle changes in atmosphere that lighting can create. The adoption nowadays of computerised lighting boards enables many complex changes to be achieved during the course of each ballet.

Mercury Ensemble

Ballet Rambert's musical range has widened enormously since it became a contemporary company. It now has a chamber orchestra called the Mercury Ensemble, which sometimes gives concerts and lectures in its own right. This is not a resident full-time orchestra, but instead musicians are employed as required for the ballets in the current repertory. Today all the music is played live wherever possible, the only exceptions being electronic sound scores or specially taped effects, where recordings are used. The musicians and singers who perform with the Mercury Ensemble have to cope with the demands of a broad spectrum of musical styles, from classical to avant-garde, and including folk, jazz and rock. For example in the 1981 repertory the string quintet first played gentle, lyrical music by Vaugham Williams and then turned their hands to George Crumb's modern score, *Black Angels*, with its aggressive and unusual sounds produced on the same instruments.

John Chesworth

John Chesworth was appointed artistic director for Ballet Rambert in 1974, following Norman Morrice's departure. He had trained at the Rambert School and joined the company in 1952, becoming a fine character dancer in productions such as *Don Quixote*. In 1966 Chesworth was made assistant to the directors, and took on much of the work of reorganising the company. In 1970 he was made associate director. He choreographed seven ballets for the new company, for both workship and main seasons. These included *Time Base, H*, an anti-war piece, and *Ad Hoc*, which introduced the idea of having the dancers improvise to instructions given to them on stage.

As director, Chesworth continued Morrice's policies, encouraging creative work from the company and inviting guest choreographers to broaden the repertory. Americans Glen Tetley, Cliff Keuter and Sara Sugihara and the Dutch choreographer Jaap Flier all made new works for Ballet Rambert. Chesworth also invited Robert North, Micha Bergese and Siobhan Davies, all members of London Contemporary Dance Theatre, to choreograph. Two further workshop seasons, *Collaborations III and IV*, were given in association with students from the Central School of Art and Design. From 1978 Ballet Rambert has presented annual workshop seasons at Riverside Studios, an arts centre in Hammersmith. Outstanding dancers this time were Lucy Burge, Christopher Bruce, Zoltan Imre, Sally Owen and Leigh Warren. In addition to Bruce, the last three named also choreographed for the main company repertory.

Chesworth was keenly interested in expanding Ballet Rambert's presentation of contemporary dance to encompass large-scale productions. During his directorship two full-length works were produced, Bruce's *Cruel Garden* in 1977 and Tetley's *The Tempest* in 1979. Both of these productions stretched the company's resources to the full. They involved large-scale sets and many costumes, had specially commissioned musical scores, and used the company's full complement of eighteen dancers, many of whom had to perform several different roles during the course of each ballet. Fortunately both *Cruel Garden* and *The Tempest* have been very successful with audiences.

Chesworth was particularly concerned to develop Ballet Rambert's educational activities, and under his guidance this aspect of the company's work continued to grow. In 1975 various company members choreographed a new children's show, called *Take a Running Jump*. This was informative as well as being great fun. It showed the dancers training and looked at the history of ballet as well as introducing some works from the repertory. In 1979 Chesworth produced *Inside The Tempest*, an introduction to Tetley's ballet, which explained the choregraphy, music and design and showed extracts in performance. This format has been adapted for successive programmes, *Inside the Repertoire* in 1980 and *What's in a Dance?* in 1982, both of which aimed at giving young people an understanding of the choreography and staging of modern dance theatre. John Chesworth left Ballet Rambert in 1980, having directed the company for six years.

New developments and changes

Rambert Academy
It had been felt for some time that Ballet Rambert would benefit from having its own training school closely linked to the company, as in previous times. So in 1979 the Rambert Academy was set up as a joint venture with the West London Institute of Higher Education, at Twickenham in Middlesex. This offers a professional training in classical ballet and contemporary dance and the opportunity to study for G.C.E. 'A' level in several subjects at the Institute. The Academy was directed first by Gary Sherwood, who was formerly a dancer with The Royal Ballet and ballet master for Ballet Rambert. Already students from the Academy have performed during main company seasons in London and Bristol, and choreographers Robert North, Christopher Bruce and Richard Alston have worked with the students and made ballets for them. Meanwhile the independently run Rambert School of Ballet continued to prosper under the direction of Angela and David Ellis, and in 1979 expansion forced the Upper School to move into studios at The Place, home of the London Contemporary Dance School.

Ballet Rambert School
It was finally decided to combine the two schools bearing the Rambert name. In 1982 the Upper Rambert School moved into extended studio space at Twickenham and from 1983 it began to merge its students with those from the Academy. The Princess of Wales attended a fund-raising gala which Ballet Rambert held on the first night of its Sadler's Wells season in March 1983. This gala helped to raise money for the new studios and for scholarships which could be offered to some of the students. The new training school thus formed is called the Ballet Rambert School. It continues to develop a close relationship with the Ballet Rambert company.

43

Richard Alston

In the 1980s the creative team leading Ballet Rambert was strengthened by two new arrivals. The first of these was Richard Alston, who joined as resident choreographer in 1980, having already created *Bell High* for the company. Alston was an early member of London Contemporary Dance Theatre and then left to form his own company, Strider, and to work as a free-lance choreographer. Since joining Ballet Rambert he has made several new ballets, including *Rainbow Ripples, The Rite of Spring*, a new version of the ballet that Marie Rambert had worked on with Nijinsky almost seventy years before, *Apollo Distraught* and *Chicago Brass*. Having himself an art school background, Alston is interested in presenting his choreography in association with visual art. In 1981 he made *Soda Lake*, which is a solo dance constructed around a sculpture by Nigel Hall, for a workshop season at Riverside Studios. Later in the same year he made *Night Music*, for which the designs were created by the contemporary painter Howard Hodgkin.

Richard Alston's Rainbow Ripples, *1980. Dancers from left to right: Cathrine Price, Catherine Becque and Rebecca Ham. Backcloth designed by David Buckland.*
Photo: Anthony Crickmay.

Robert North

The second arrival was Robert North, who became Ballet Rambert's new artistic director in 1981. North was born in the United States and trained at the Royal Ballet School before joining London Contemporary Dance Theatre. He also danced with the Martha Graham Company before returning to LCDT, where he became a leading dancer and choreographer. As a guest choreographer, he had already made *Running Figures* and *Reflections* for Ballet Rambert. North is continuing his career as a dancer and choreographer as well as directing the company. His new works for Ballet Rambert are *Lonely Town, Lonely Street*, which is danced in jazz style to soul music by the American Bill Withers, and *Pribaoutki*, whose title means 'nonsense verse' in Russian, which brings to life characters from Picasso paintings and is set to songs by Stravinsky. In 1983 he made *Colour Moves*, which is danced to a series of strikingly coloured backcloths designed by a leading British fine artist, Bridget Riley. North is concerned with preserving the classical foundations of the company and he considers it especially important that Ballet Rambert should continue to be a strongly musical company. At the same time he has expressed a commitment to the Rambert policy of being experimental and encouraging new creative talent.

Ballet Rambert today

In 1976 Ballet Rambert, the oldest British dance company, celebrated its fiftieth birthday. The Victoria and Albert Theatre Museum commemorated the occasion with a special exhibition on the company's history, and Ballet Rambert gave a gala performance at Sadler's Wells Theatre. As a tribute to Marie Rambert, Christopher Bruce created for her a new ballet, *Girl with Straw Hat*, which began with dancer Sally Owen impersonating Rambert in a pose from a well-known photograph. This shows Rambert as a schoolgirl in Warsaw, wearing a satchel and firmly clutching one of her favourite possessions, a huge straw hat. The choreography matched the exuberance of Marie Rambert herself, and included some of her famous cartwheels.

After restarting in 1966, Ballet Rambert has developed into a leading modern dance company with an international reputation once again. It continues to produce talented dancers, choreographers and directors for other dance companies in Britain and throughout the world. Foreign visits have in recent years included, France, Italy, Germany, Holland, Belgium, Luxemburg, Greece, Czechosolvakia, Bulgaria, Romania, Yugoslavia, Hungary and Israel, and an extensive tour of the United States in autumn 1982. By 1982 the annual grant from the Arts Council of Great Britain had risen to over half a million pounds. This financial support commits the company to touring in Britain for approximately half the year, but also enables it to spend much of the rest of the time on creative work, producing five or six new ballets every year. Most of these are choreographed by company members, although other leading choreographers are occasionally invited to contribute to the repertory. For example the work of three Americans has recently been featured. Paul Taylor's *Airs* was remounted for the company in 1982. In 1983 Merce Cunningham, who for over a generation has pioneered the avant-garde in dance, gave the company *Fielding Sixes*. Later in 1983 Glen Tetley returned, after an absence of several years, to create *Murderer Hope of Women* for Ballet Rambert's first ever visit to the Edinburgh International Festival in August of that year.

In 1983 Ballet Rambert restaged three ballets from its past, in tribute to its late founder, Marie Rambert. The works were chosen for their particular historical significance. These were, first, Nijinsky's *L'Après-midi d'un Faune*, originally created in 1912 for Diaghilev's Ballets Russes. Rambert danced in the original production as one of the nymphs. The second work was an early ballet by Frederick Ashton, *Capriol Suite*, which was made for the Marie Rambert Dancers in 1930. Former Rambert ballerinas Elisabeth Schooling and Sally Gilmour returned to the company to remount *Capriol Suite*, which they had danced in so many years before. The third work to be restaged was Ashton's *Five Brahms Waltzes in the Manner of Isadora Duncan*, which he created in 1976 from his memories of having seen Duncan dance when he was a young man. The Isadora Duncan waltzes acknowledge the immense inspiration that Isadora's dancing had for both Ashton and Marie Rambert.

The company today is mostly very different in terms of the dance it presents from when it began in the 1920s and 30s, and no doubt it is completely different from what Marie Rambert might have envisaged then. Nevertheless in many ways its artistic policies are still very close to those of the early days and the creative atmosphere of the Ballet Club has been regenerated. Ballet Rambert has made a large contribution to the building of a wide audience for contemporary dance in this country since the 1960s. By reaching out particularly to young people through its performances and its educational activities Ballet Rambert has also played a major part in the huge growth in popularity that dance has enjoyed in recent years in Britain.

The sad death in 1982 of Marie Rambert, the company's founder, was seen by many people as marking the end of an era for dance in this country. Ballet Rambert enters the 1980s under the directorship of Robert North, which may well see some changes, but to quote a statement made by Norman Morrice and Marie Rambert in 1966, 'A company cannot stand still if it is to safeguard the future'.

Suggested Further Reading

Austin, R. (1976) *Birth of a ballet*. London: Vision.

* Clarke, M. (1962) *Dancers of Mercury*. London: A. & C. Black.

Crisp, P., Sainsbury, A. and Williams, P. (Eds.) (1981) *Ballet Rambert: 50 years and on*. London: Mercury Theatre Trust.

Murray, J. (1979) *Dance now*. Harmondsworth: Penguin.

Rambert, M. (1983) *Quicksilver. London: MacMillan*.

* Now out of print but well worth searching for in second-hand bookshops or your local library.

Ballet Rambert:
Chart showing signficant events in the history of the company

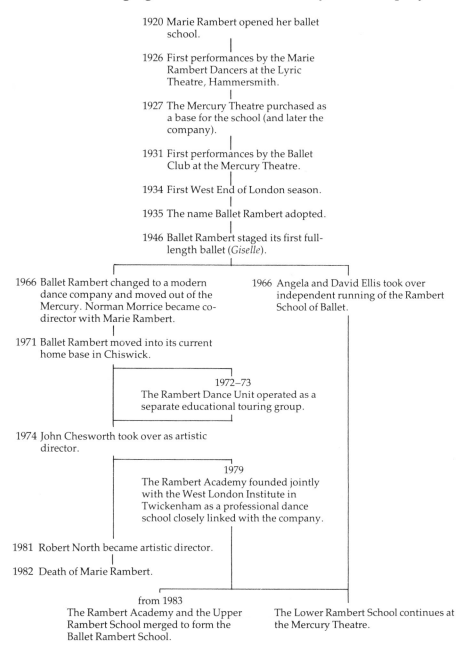

1920 Marie Rambert opened her ballet school.

1926 First performances by the Marie Rambert Dancers at the Lyric Theatre, Hammersmith.

1927 The Mercury Theatre purchased as a base for the school (and later the company).

1931 First performances by the Ballet Club at the Mercury Theatre.

1934 First West End of London season.

1935 The name Ballet Rambert adopted.

1946 Ballet Rambert staged its first full-length ballet (*Giselle*).

1966 Ballet Rambert changed to a modern dance company and moved out of the Mercury. Norman Morrice became co-director with Marie Rambert.

1966 Angela and David Ellis took over independent running of the Rambert School of Ballet.

1971 Ballet Rambert moved into its current home base in Chiswick.

1972–73
The Rambert Dance Unit operated as a separate educational touring group.

1974 John Chesworth took over as artistic director.

1979
The Rambert Academy founded jointly with the West London Institute in Twickenham as a professional dance school closely linked with the company.

1981 Robert North became artistic director.

1982 Death of Marie Rambert.

from 1983
The Rambert Academy and the Upper Rambert School merged to form the Ballet Rambert School.

The Lower Rambert School continues at the Mercury Theatre.

Ballet Rambert: Choreochronicle of works mentioned in the chapter

DATE OF FIRST PERFORMANCE BY BALLET RAMBERT	TITLE	CHOREOGRAPHER	COMPOSER	DESIGNER	DATE OF FIRST PERFORMANCE IF ORIGINALLY PRODUCED ELSEWHERE
1926	A Tragedy of Fashion	Ashton	E. Goossens	Fedorovitch	
1930	Capriol Suite	Ashton	Warlock	Chappell	
1930	Les Sylphides	Fokine	Chopin		First performed under the title *Les Sylphides* by Diaghilev's Ballets Russes, 1909
1930	Le Rugby	Salaman	Poulenc	Salaman	
1930	Le Spectre de la Rose	Fokine	Weber	Bakst (costumes)	Diaghilev's Ballets Russes, 1911,
1930	Le Carnaval	Fokine	Schumann	Bakst (costumes)	Diaghilev's Ballets Russes, 1910
1930	Le Cricket	Salaman	Benjamin	Salaman	
1931	Le Boxing	Salaman	Berners	Chappell	
1931	La Péri	Ashton	Dukas	Chappell	
1931	Aurora's Wedding (excerpts from The Sleeping Beauty)	Petipa	Tchaikovsky	Bakst	Imperial Russian Ballet, 1890
1931	L'Après-midi d'un Faune	Nijinsky	Debussy		Diahilev's Ballets Russes, 1912
1931	Le Lac des Cygnes (Adagio)	Petipa/Ivanov	Tchaikovsky		Imperial Russian Ballet, 1895
1932	Foyer de Danse	Ashton	Berners	Chappell after Degas	
1933	Les Masques	Ashton	Poulenc	Fedorovitch	
1934	Mermaid	Howard/Salaman	Ravel	Howard	
1934	Bar aux Folies-Bergère	de Valois	Chabrier	Chappell after Manet	
1934	Mephisto Valse	Ashton	Liszt	Fedorovitch	
1934	The Planets	Tudor	Holst	Stevenson	
1935	Cinderella	Howard	Weber	Howard	
1936	Jardin aux Lilas (Lilac Garden)	Tudor	Chausson	Stevenson	
1937	Dark Elegies	Tudor	Mahler	Nadia Benois	
1937	Death and the Maiden	Howard	Schubert	Howard	
1937	Le Lac des Cygnes (Act II)	Petipa/Ivanov	Tchaikovsky		Imperial Russian Ballet, 1895
1939	Lady into Fox	Howard	Honegger	Nadia Benois	
1939	Czernyana	Staff	Czerny	Swinstead-Smith	
1940	Judgment of Paris	Tudor	Weill	Laing	London Ballet, 1938

DATE OF FIRST PERFORMANCE BY BALLET RAMBERT	TITLE	CHOREOGRAPHER	COMPOSER	DESIGNER	DATE OF FIRST PERFORMANCE IF ORIGINALLY PRODUCED ELSEWHERE
1940	Peter and the Wolf	Staff	Prokofiev	Sheppard	
1946	Mr. Punch	Gore	Oldham	Wilson	
1946	Giselle	Coralli/Perrot	Adam	Stevenson	Paris Opéra, 1841
1947	The Sailor's Return	Howard	Oldham	Howard	
1948	Nutcracker Suite (The Nutcracker Act II)	Ivanov	Tchaikovsky	Cordwell	Imperial Russian Ballet, 1892
1955	Laiderette	MacMillan	Martin	Rowell	Sadler's Wells Group, 1954
1957	Coppélia	Ivanov after Saint-Léon	Delibes	Doboujinksy	Original production by Saint-Léon for Paris Opéra, 1870; Petipa version, attributed in England to Ivanov, St. Petersburg, 1894
1958	Two Brothers	Morrice	Dohnanyi	Koltai	
1960	La Sylphide	Bournonville staged by von Rosen	Lovenskjold	C. and R. Ironside	Original Bournonville production for Royal Danish Ballet, 1836
1962	Don Quixote	Gorsky/Zakharov staged by Borkowski	Minkus	Voytek	Original production by Petipa for Imperial Russian Ballet, 1869; Gorsky production for Imperial Russian Ballet, 1900; Zakharov production for Bolshoi Ballet, 1940
1963	Les Sylphides	Fokine	Chopin	Stone	As for 1930 production
1965	Giselle	Coralli/Perrot/Petipa	Adam	Farmer	As for 1946 production
1967	Time Base	Chesworth	Lutoslawski	Baylis	
1967	Pierrot Lunaire	Tetley	Schoenberg	Ter-Arutunian	Glen Tetley and Company, 1962
1967	Ricercare	Tetley	Seter	Ter-Arutunian	American Ballet Theatre, 1966
1967	Collaboration I	various	various	Central School of Art and Design	
1967	Freefall	Tetley	Schubel	Tetley	Repertory Dance Theatre, University of Utah, 1967
1967	Ziggurat	Tetley	Stockhausen	Baylis	
1968	'H'	Chesworth	Penderecki	Chesworth	
1968	Collaboration II	various	various	Central School of Art and Design	

Year	Title	Choreographer	Music	Design	Notes
1968	Embrace Tiger and Return to Mountain	Tetley	Subotnik	Baylis	
1969	George Frideric	Bruce	Handel	Napier	
1969	Blind Sight	Morrice	Downes	Baylis	
1970	Bertram Batell's Sideshow	various	various	Cazalet	
1971	That is the Show	Morrice	Berio	Baylis	
1971	Rag Dances	Tetley	Hymas	Baylis	
1972	Dance for New Dimensions	various	various	Baylis	
1972	'for these who die as cattle'	Bruce			
1972	Ad Hoc	Chesworth	improvised		
1973	Dance for New Dimensions	various	various	various	
1975	Running Figures	North	Burgon	Farmer	
1975	Ancient Voices of Children	Bruce	Crumb	Baylis	
1975	Take a Running Jump	various	various	Murray-Clark	
1976	Collaboration III	various	various	Central School of Art and Design	
1976	Black Angels	Bruce	Crumb	Baylis	
1976	Reflections	North	Blake	Baylis	
1976	Girl with Straw Hat	Bruce	Brahms	Baylis	
1977	Collaboration IV	various	various	Central School of Art and Design	
1977	Smiling Immortal	Morrice	Harvey	Macfarlane	
1977	Cruel Garden	Bruce/Kemp	Miranda	Koltai/Kemp	
1978	Praeludium	Tetley	Webern	Baylis	
1979	The Tempest	Tetley	Nordheim	Baylis	
1979	Night With Waning Moon	Bruce	Crumb	Marre	
1980	Bell High	Alston	Maxwell Davies	Mumford	
1980	Preludes and Song	Bruce	Hymas	Marre	
1980	Rainbow Ripples	Alston	Amirkhanian/Green	Buckland	
1981	The Rite of Spring	Alston	Stravinsky	Mumford/Guyon	Original version choreographed by Nijinsky for Diaghilev's Ballets Russes, 1913
1981	Ghost Dances	Bruce	South American folk music	Bruce/Scarlett	
1981	Lonely Town, Lonely Street	North	Withers	Storer	The Janet Smith Dance Group, 1980

DATE OF FIRST PERFORMANCE BY BALLET RAMBERT	TITLE	CHOREOGRAPHER	COMPOSER	DESIGNER	DATE OF FIRST PERFORMANCE IF ORIGINALLY PRODUCED ELSEWHERE
1981	Night Music	Alston	Mozart	Hodgkin	
1982	Requiem	Bruce	Brecht/Weill	Marre	
1982	Airs	Taylor	Handel	Moore	The Paul Taylor Dance Company, 1978
1982	Pribaoutki	North	Stravinsky	Storer after Picasso	
1982	Apollo Distraught	Alston	Osborne	Mumford/Cook	
1983	Chicago Brass	Alston	Hindermith	Alston	
1983	Fielding Sixes	Cunningham	Cage	Lancaster	Merce Cunningham Company, 1980
1983	Five Brahms Waltzes in the Manner of Isadora Duncan	Ashton	Brahms	Dean	Ballet Rambert Gala, 1976
1983	Murderer Hope of Women	Tetley	Tyrrell	Baylis	
1983	Colour Moves	North	Benstead	Riley/Storer	

A complete list of works danced by Ballet Rambert may be found in Crisp, C. Sainsbury, A. and Williams, P. (Eds.) (1981) *Ballet Rambert: 50 years and on.* London: Mercury Theatre Trust.

Chapter 2

The Royal Ballet and Sadler's Wells Royal Ballet

Werdon Anglin

The Royal Ballet and Sadler's Wells Royal Ballet are Britain's national ballet. Together with the Royal Ballet School, they comprise one of the most important and best-known centres of classical dance in the world. Yet little more than fifty years ago there was no British national ballet and the idea that British dancers could become world-famous was considered impossible, even absurd, by most people. How then, did this great change come about in such a comparatively short time? This chapter provides the answer and tells the story of The Royal Ballet from the 1920s, when it began, until today. It can be divided into four distinct sections:

1920–63　　the formation and early development of the company under its founder Ninette de Valois;

1963–70　　the consolidation of the company under Frederick Ashton;

1970–　　　new developments under the direction of Kenneth MacMillan, followed by Norman Morrice;

1946–　　　Sadler's Wells Royal Ballet.

Ballet in Britain today began with the foundation of two schools of classical ballet: one by Marie Rambert, the Rambert School, in 1920; the other by Ninette de Valois, the Academy of Choreographic Art, in 1926. The latter is, today, the Royal Ballet School.

But ballet in Britain actually has a much longer history than this; something like three hundred years, mostly in the form of visits and performances by famous dancers and companies from Europe.

A history of visiting dancers and companies, however, is not the same thing as having a native ballet tradition with British schools and British dancers. So, if you wanted to start such a tradition how would you set about it? Most people would look around for examples outside Britain, learning from others. Essentially, this is what happened in the 1920s although it was not planned consciously this way.

In the 1920s the eyes of anyone interested in classical ballet were fixed on the famous Ballets Russes of Serge Diaghilev, and on the company which toured with the great Russian ballerina Anna Pavlova. Between them, these two companies dominated the international ballet scene. Both used British dancers, amongst them names which are famous today, such as Ninette de Valois, Alicia Markova, and Anton Dolin.

The magic of Russian ballet was so strong and the idea that Britain could develop its own ballet tradition seemed so remote that British dancers adopted Russian or foreign names in order to build their careers. Thus Alicia Markova was really Alicia Marks, Anton Dolin was born Patrick Healey-Kay, and Ninette de Valois was Irish-born Edris Stannus.

Many factors, however, combined to bring teachers and dancers from abroad to settle in Britain, strengthening the good schools and teachers already here. One of the personalities from abroad was Marie Rambert, a Polish dancer who married the English playwright, Ashley Dukes, and settled in London. Her background is described fully in the chapter on Ballet Rambert. What is important to us here is that she opened a school in 1920 and in 1926 her students appeared in a revue *Riverside Nights*, at the Lyric Theatre, Hammersmith, London. For this revue, one of her students, Frederick Ashton, created a short ballet, *A Tragedy of Fashion*, appearing in it with Rambert herself. In this way, *A Tragedy of Fashion* became the first English ballet of modern times.

The formation and early development of the company unders its founder, Ninette de Valois

The Foundation of a school

While Rambert was starting her school in London, Ninette de Valois was dancing with Diaghilev's company, learning the repertory of its famous ballets and learning how to organise, direct, and administer the complex human mixture which is a ballet company.

Her own background had prepared her very well for this. By 1923 when she entered Diaghilev's company she had been dancing professionally for nearly ten years, mostly as principal dancer. She had absorbed from the two great teachers Espinosa and Cecchetti the principles of the French and Italian schools of ballet, especially the Italian enshrined in the teaching method of Cecchetti, one of the greatest teachers in the history of classical ballet. Not surprisingly, therefore, she became a soloist with Diaghilev's company and could have gone on to a fine career as a dancer. It surprised many when she gave up her opportunities with Diaghilev and returned to England in 1925 to open a year later a ballet school which she called the Academy of Choreographic Art, a name suggested by the ballet historian Cyril Beaumont.

The year 1926 is a landmark in the history of British ballet, for four reasons:

(1) It marked the creation of the first English ballet of modern times, *A Tragedy of Fashion*.
(2) It marked the opening of an Academy of Dance which has become the Royal Ballet School.
(3) It was the year that de Valois met Lilian Baylis, the manager of the Old Vic Theatre in South London. This theatre already housed both a drama and an opera company and de Valois wished to add a ballet company.
(4) Finally, Ninette de Valois was recognised as a significant teacher and choreographer in her own right. Lilian Baylis was interested in the de Valois plan for a ballet company at the Old Vic, and, as a beginning, engaged de Valois as a teacher of movement for actors and actresses and as choreographer for dancers in operas and plays. Time has justified

Lilian Baylis' confidence in her, for de Valois became one of the strongest influences on the teaching methods which have formed British ballet and a founding choreographer of her own company.

The Academy of Choreographic Art, and the Vic-Wells School which it became in 1931, did more than any other institution to transfer to British physiques the legacy of two centuries of ballet tradition from other European countries. From Italy, through Enrico Cecchetti, teacher of Diaghilev's Ballets Russes, came the traditions of the Italian school, brilliance of execution combined with expressiveness and musicality. From France, through Edouard Espinosa, and Denmark, through Adeline Genée, came the grace and charm and great teaching traditions of the French school. From Russia, through dancers and teachers like Nicholas Legat, Seraphine Astafieva and many others, came the grandeur and discoveries of the Russian school which combined French and Italian experience upon Russian physiques and temperaments during the latter part of the nineteenth century.

Thus all four existing national schools of ballet in Europe – French, Italian, Danish and Russian – combined to begin the creation of a fifth European school, the British, during the middle years of the twentieth century.

Throughout the next decade, British teachers aided this development through working jointly with Cecchetti, Espinosa and Genée to form three important teaching and examining organisations:

(1) the Royal Academy of Dancing;
(2) the Imperial Society of Teachers of Dancing;
(3) the British Ballet Organisation.

These organisations, by their system of examination, their schools and courses, have done much to raise the standard of teaching and dancing throughout the British Commonwealth as well as finding and fostering young talent for Britain's new professional dance companies.

The Emergence of a Company

By the end of the 1920s the teaching structure for ballet in Britain, and the foundations of its first two companies, the Vic-Wells Ballet and the Marie Rambert Dancers, had been laid. Each of the companies created its own works, seeking to realise the dream of the British dance world, a British ballet.

On 19 August 1929, the sudden death of Diaghilev, creator of the Ballets Russes and ballet's central inspiration, threatened to dissolve that dream. However, in Britain, those who shared the dream of a British ballet came together to preserve and advance what had been achieved already. This led to the formation of the Camargo Society, a subscription society commited to presenting good quality classical ballet in London's West End. This would not have been possible without the strong teaching basis which existed by that time and which was to be the key to the story which follows. The important dance stars were mostly Russian dancers like Lydia Lopokova, Olga Spessivtseva and the Russian-trained Alicia Markova. But the venture could not have succeeded without dancers from the schools of de Valois and Rambert.

Its first performance was at the Cambridge Theatre, London, 19 October 1930. Between then and 1933, when the Society closed, its aim accomplished, it had produced sixteen ballets in addition to revivals of shortened versions of *Swan Lake, Giselle* and *Coppélia*. During its time it made a point of commissioning music, costumes and décor from well-known or promising British artists, thus helping to link the emerging national ballet with British tradition in music and the visual arts.

The Society had the foresight to close as soon as de Valois' Vic-Wells Ballet and Ballet Rambert were strong enough to stand alone, and the ballets the Camargo Society had stimulated were incorporated in their respective repertories. Amongst these were Frederick Ashton's *Capriol Suite* and *Façade*, and *Job* by Ninette de Valois to music by Vaughan Williams.

Thus the emerging British ballet embraced not only British physiques and temperaments, but also British composers, poets, designers and choreographers. In this way, the Camargo Society silenced those who said that a British ballet could not be formed from truly British ingredients.

The largest of these ingredients was the company directed by de Valois in Lilian Baylis' Old Vic Theatre, South London. But the Old Vic was proving too small to house a drama, opera *and* ballet company. So the next great need was a permanent home in some other theatre which would permit regular ballet performances. Baylis had her eyes already on Sadler's Wells Theatre in Islington. Her idea was a people's theatre north of the Thames, matching the Old Vic, south of the river. Opera, ballet, and the works of Shakespeare, were to be presented in both theatres.

During 1930 the dilapidated Sadler's Wells Theatre was rebuilt, and reopened on Twelfth Night, 1931. At the same time, de Valois transferred to it her school and the Vic-Wells Ballet, then a little company of six dancers.

At first the Vic-Wells appeared in opera productions at the Old Vic and Sadler's Wells Theatre, but presently the management decided it might risk a whole evening of ballet. This carefully planned performance took place on the evening of 5 May 1931, the date regarded ever since as the birthday of the company. It was a spectacular success. So much so that other performances followed and ballet soon became a regular part of the theatre's programme.

Early Repertory

Regular performances required the creation of new works a repertory of classical and contemporary ballets. Fokine's *Les Sylphides*, for example, was introduced in March 1932, led by Alicia Markova and Anton Dolin. The following year Frederick Ashton created *Les Rendezvous*. Again, Markova danced the leading role but her

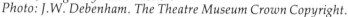

Alicia Markova as the Betrayed Girl in the first performance of The Rake's Progress, *20 May 1935. Music by Gavin Gordon, choreography by Ninette de Valois, designs by Rex Whistler.*
Photo: J.W. Debenham. The Theatre Museum Crown Copyright.

partner was a Polish dancer, Stanislas Idzikowski, another leading dancer from the Diaghilev company. The inclusion of ballets and dancers from Diaghilev's Ballets Russes meant that the growing repertory was linked firmly with the Russian tradition. Ashton's *Les Rendezvous* showed too the beginning of an emerging English classical style. Its qualities were neatness, speed and precision, combined with a talent for detailed characterisation. Ninette de Valois particularly developed this talent through the dramatic ballets she created for the growing company. Most famous of these was *The Rake's Progress*. It remains today one of the most popular ballets in the repertory, based on William Hogarth's masterpiece and created to music by Gavin Gordon with scenery and costumes by Rex Whistler, one of the most famous artists of the day. Thus de Valois combined her practice of using English collaborators and drawing on English tradition.

The Rake's Progress in 1935 marked the end of one phase, the beginning of another, for the Vic-Wells Ballet. In it, Alicia Markova, as the Betrayed Girl, created her last role at Sadler's Wells Theatre. With Anton Dolin, she left to form their own company and move on to the international stage. For two years she had played a very important role in the development of the company. Her presence as the Vic-Wells ballerina made possible in that time the first British productions of the great classics *Giselle, Swan Lake* and *The Nutcracker*. These were produced in full versions for the first time during 1934, helping to develop the company's dancing power and absorb more of the heritage of the past. They were mounted for de Valois by Nicholas Sergeyev, a Russian dancer and ballet master who had been régisseur-général of the Imperial Ballet in St. Petersburg until he left Russia in 1918.

Such a development could take place only through British dancers trained in a British school, dancing works created by British choreographers, however strong their debt to other classical schools.

The year 1935 was also significant because Margot Fonteyn, one of the first products of the young Vic-Wells School, was appointed to follow Alicia Markova as the company ballerina. Frederick Ashton joined the company full-time as resident choreographer, thus completing the team which would build The Royal Ballet – de Valois, Ashton, and Constant Lambert; de Valois as leader and organiser, Ashton as choreographer and Lambert as musical guide and director. Lambert, whom de Valois had met during her days with Diaghilev, had joined the tiny Vic-Wells company in 1931 and became responsible for its musical life. Others alongside Fonteyn in this first generation of British-trained dancers were Robert Helpmann, Harold Turner, Michael Somes, Pamela May, June Brae, Beryl Grey and later Moira Shearer.

As resident choreographer, Ashton became not only the creator of countless works, but also the man chiefly responsible for creating what is now known as the English style of classical ballet. His ballets moulded the dancers technically and artistically, always challenging them to do more as dancers, as artists, and as characters. All these qualities are evident in his *Apparitions* and *Les Patineurs*, both created for the company in the 1930s.

These, along with the de Valois dramatic ballets like *Checkmate* and *The Rake's Progress*, plus the big classical works, provided the schooling and challenges all dancers need.

The last of these big classics to enter the repertory was *The Sleeping Princess* in February 1939, made possible by an extension of the stage of Sadler's Wells Theatre, paid for by public subscription as a memorial to Lilian Baylis who had died in November 1937. This was the company's last major production before war broke out in September 1939.

1939–45: The war years

As with the British way of life in general, the war changed the context in which the Vic-Wells Ballet worked. It entered the war as a relatively small successful company supported by a loyal and growing London audience. When the war ended it had won a national audience and was accepted as Britain's national ballet company. This was largely because the constant touring to factories, training camps and bases, as well as theatres of all kinds, as part of the war effort, introduced ballet to thousands of people who had never seen the art before. On the occasions when the company danced in London, thousands of servicemen and other visitors to the capital saw it and took back with them the memory of Sadler's Wells Ballet, the name the company adopted in 1941.

Touring conditions were harsh and the beginning was made worse by the decision of the Foreign Office to send the company to Holland only days before that country was invaded by Hitler in May 1940. The company itself escaped with only hours to spare, but they had to leave behind the scenery, costumes and all the music and orchestral parts of six ballets; a bitter loss at any time but particularly so when rationing of clothing and materials made replacement almost impossible.

Apart from the difficulties of living and dancing in wartime Britain, the blackout, rationing and air-raids during performances, the company's greatest problem was lack of male dancers. Almost all the first generation of male dancers was conscripted, except Robert Helpmann, an Australian. In this way the war cemented the famous Fonteyn/Helpmann partnership which was partly responsible for stimulating the popularity ballet then won. When Ashton was called up, de Valois needed to find quickly another choreographer, and this too Helpmann became. *Hamlet*, his most famous work, condensed the main events of Shakespeare's play as they might have emerged in the brain of the dying Hamlet, unable to separate one image from another.

In *Hamlet*, and his other ballets for the company, *Comus*, *Miracle in the Gorbals*, and later, *Adam Zero*, Helpmann exploited the mime and acting element in ballet and the gifts of characterisation which are such an important part of British dancing.

The war-time tours of Sadler's Wells Ballet were made possible by the Council for the Encouragement of Music and the Arts, formed to bring the arts to every corner of Britain to sustain morale by amusing, entertaining and reminding people of values for which they were fighting. The Council had so proved its worth that at the end of the war it was transformed into the Arts Council of Great Britain. With its help, the Sadler's Wells Ballet was also transformed. When war ended in 1945 and the male dancers returned home, the company briefly re-entered its home theatre in Islington. The Royal Opera House, Covent Garden, too, ceased its wartime job of being a dance-hall for troops. For some time plans had been prepared to make it a permanent centre of lyric theatre so that it was natural that Sadler's Wells Ballet should provide the dance element of such a vision.

1946–63: The move to Covent Garden and the formation of a second company

In 1946 the company moved to Covent Garden. On 20th February of that year, in the presence of the Royal Family, the red and gold curtain of the Royal Opera House rose for the first time on a new production of the same ballet which Ninette de Valois had discussed with Lilian Baylis before her death in 1937, *The Sleeping*

Beauty. This production of the ballet was immensely successful and became the hallmark of the company in the immediate post-war years. It provided also the centre-piece around which the company was reformed and matured in the ten years from its production in 1946 to the granting of a Royal Charter in 1956. No less significantly it was the production with which Sadler's Wells Ballet and Margot Fonteyn conquered New York in 1949 and so won international recognition to add to the national recognition won during the war.

The move to Covent Garden meant that another smaller company was needed at Sadler's Wells Theatre, at least to appear in the productions of Sadler's Wells Opera. Such a company also could help bring forward talent needed to sustain the much larger demands now made on Sadler's Wells Ballet at the Royal Opera House.

The new company became known as Sadler's Wells Theatre Ballet. Its story is told separately at the end of this chapter, along with the stories of the Royal Ballet Touring Company and Sadler's Wells Royal Ballet, which are its descendants.

It is significant to the larger company's history, however, because its smaller size enabled it to find and develop more quickly choreographers of the calibre of John Cranko and Kenneth MacMillan, and dancers who were to win international recognition such as Svetlana Beriosova, Nadia Nerina and David Blair.

The year 1956, the year Sadler's Wells Ballet received its Royal Charter form the Queen and became The Royal Ballet, is a good moment to review what had been achieved since 1931 and to glance forward.

There now existed two companies, The Royal Ballet at Covent Garden and a large touring company. There was also the Royal Ballet School, well-established and producing the dancers of tomorrow. All these organisations were linked together and their future safe-guarded under the provision of the Royal Charter. This, much more than the new title 'The Royal Ballet', is the real significance of the Charter.

If you were asked to study and assess a dance company, how would you go about it? You should look at its repertory of ballets, its dancers, its choreographers, teaching methods and policy. This, briefly, is how we are going to examine The Royal Ballet between 1956 and 1963, when its founder, Dame Ninette de Valois, retired.

Henry Danton, Moira Shearer, Michael Somes, Margot Fonteyn, Pamela May and Brian Shaw in Symphonic Variations, *24 April 1946. This was Frederick Ashton's first ballet for the company after its move to the Royal Opera House. Music by César Franck, designs by Sophie Fedorovitch.*
Photo: Baron

Choreographers

In 1956 the company was internationally famous and had two very experienced choreographers in de Valois and Ashton, whose ballets were part of the foundation of the company. These ballets were important in developing a genuinely British dancing style and in challenging and developing dancers.

Amongst de Valois' ballets were *Job*, *The Rake's Progress* and *Checkmate*. Ashton was represented by *Les Rendezvous*, *Façade*, *Les Patineurs*, *Symphonic Variations* and *Cinderella*.

The company had also two very promising new choreographers in John Cranko from South Africa and Kenneth MacMillan from Scotland. Already Cranko had created ballets like *Pineapple Poll*, *Beauty and the Beast* and *The Lady and the Fool*.

MacMillan's early work included *Danses Concertantes*, still in the repertory of Sadler's Wells Royal Ballet.

The rest of the repertory consisted mainly of the great classics, *Swan Lake*, *The Sleeping Beauty*, *Giselle*, *Coppélia*, and *The Nut-*

cracker, alongside ballets inherited from Diaghilev's Ballets Russes such as Fokine's *Les Sylphides* and *The Firebird*, and Massine's *The Three-Cornered Hat*. These ballets were popular with the public and, just as importantly, their requirements of brilliant technique and special style served to train the dancers and provide a constant model for young dancers in the Royal Ballet School. Finally, the repertory was beginning to take in ballets by famous contemporary choreographers of classical ballet like *Ballet Imperial* by George Balanchine, already established as the most important person in ballet in the United States of America.

Through all this inheritance of twenty-five years since 1931 it could be said that a clear British style of classical ballet was emerging. This means that all foreign experience described at the beginning of this chapter was being absorbed into British physiques and temperaments and into British teaching methods to create British dancers dancing in a way which best suited their national temperament. Thus a new, fifth, national school of classical ballet was joining the established four in France, Italy, Denmark and Russia. This becomes particularly clear if one considers the dancers beginning to make their names at this time, such as Lynn Seymour, Merle Park, Antoinette Sibley, Donald MacLeary and Christopher Gable.

The seven years between the granting of a Royal Charter in 1956 and the retirement of de Valois in 1963 saw five very important events each one significant in the development of the company, alongside the day-to-day work of classes, rehearsals, and performances. They are:

(1) The beginning of a modification of classical style by the introduction of modern movements symbolised by the première of Kenneth MacMillan's *Agon* in August 1958. Since then the combination of classical and modern movement has gone much further, often transmitted through MacMillan's work up to and including his most recent full-length ballet, *Isadora*.

(2) The establishment of MacMillan as a choreographer of exceptional quality, the probable successor to de Valois and Ashton. His ballets *The Invitation* choreographed in 1960 and *The Rite of Spring* choreographed in 1962 particularly helped to confirm his reputation.

(3) The debut of Rudolf Nureyev with The Royal Ballet in February 1962 and the beginning of the famous Fonteyn and Nureyev partnership. This partnership was important for

Fonteyn, extending her dancing life by almost ten years. However, the real importance of Nureyev's presence in The Royal Ballet was the way in which it focused public attention on the male dancer. This did a great deal to help remove the lingering prejudice against men as ballet dancers and thus raise the status of the male dancer in public estimation. Inside the company Nureyev's technical brilliance, professionalism and standards all exerted a big influence on the male dancers so that their standards also were raised.

(4) The arrival of Eric Bruhn in the spring of 1962, marking the renewal of links with the Danish ballet, further enforced the impact of male dancing. Bruhn stayed with the company for several weeks, dancing and communicating his knowledge and Danish qualities of style to the company. In particular, an example of the work of August Bournonville, Denmark's great nineteenth-century choreographer, entered the repertory for the first time. This was in the form of a *divertissement* which included the *pas-de-deux* from *Flower Festival in Genzano* and a *pas-de-six* from *Napoli*. Bournonville favoured the male dancer in his choreography so that his very different style with its speed, attack, big jumps, deep *pliés*, *port-de-bras* and *épaulement* were another challenge to our male dancers. One of them, Anthony Dowell, particularly caught the attention as a young dancer of much promise.

(5) The Royal Ballet made its first visit to Russia, proof that the company felt strong enough to take its place on a wider international stage and to absorb what it felt was useful from other styles and ways of doing things. At the same time it continued to learn from the heritage of the past through the ballets of Diaghilev's company and also the work of Marius Petipa at the end of the nineteenth century in Russia. One of Petipa's ballets, *La Bayadère*, marked the beginning of Frederick Ashton's reign as director in 1963, and the début of Rudolph Nureyev as producer.

The consolidation of the company under Frederick Ashton, 1963–70

The company de Valois handed to Ashton had been trained in effect by both of them; she as director responsible for artistic policy, he as principal choreographer. Consequently Ashton continued most of the de Valois policies and retained the structure of the company with its two parts, one at Covent Garden, the other permanently on tour.

One of the features of Ashton's seven-year directorship, in fact, was a great strengthening of the presence of The Royal Ballet in the regions outside London. As stated earlier, when the company moved into the Royal Opera House in 1946, a much smaller company was formed at Sadler's Wells Theatre, called Sadler's Wells Theatre Ballet, to provide dancers for the opera there and also to be a proving ground for dancers and choreographers. This small company began to be developed in 1956 into a touring company large enough to mount its own productions of classics like *Swan Lake*, *Giselle* and *Coppélia*. Thus de Valois had been able to introduce the standards and repertory of The Royal Ballet into large theatres throughout Britain. Ashton continued and developed this policy.

Additionally, a small group called Ballet for All was founded in 1964 by Peter Brinson to present special programmes combining information and education on small stages in schools, halls and theatres which could not be reached by large companies. These programmes covered many aspects of ballet history. As well as basic demonstrations of the development of classical ballet technique and styles, studies of special periods were included, in particular eighteenth-century ballets reconstructed by ballet historian and choreographer Mary Skeaping, and a programme based on the original *Coppélia* of 1870. Ballet for All initially used dancers from the touring company and later both companies shared in supplying dancers for this education group.

Another feature of Ashton's directorship was the development of two famous partnerships. The one between Margot Fonteyn and Rudolf Nureyev has been mentioned already; the other was that of Antoinette Sibley and Anthony Dowell, establishing them both as artists of international importance.

A third feature of the directorship was a great enrichment of the repertory, reflecting Ashton's passionate dedication to classical

Rudolf Nureyev as Apollo with Lois Strike, Lynn Seymour and Anya Evans as the Muses in Apollo, 1975. *This ballet was first produced by Diaghilev's Ballets Russes in 1928. Music by Igor Stravinsky, choreography by George Balanchine, designs by John Craxton.*
Photo: Joe Bangay.

tradition, his attachment to French culture, his impeccable taste and continuing commitment to the classical development of The Royal Ballet and its dancers.

Mention of a few ballets, all still in the repertory, will illustrate the nature of the choreographic output of this period, 1963–70. Right at the beginning of Ashton's time as director, Rudolf Nureyev reproduced scenes from one of Petipa's great classical ballets called *La Bayadère*. This displayed in particular, the classicism and quality of The Royal Ballet's *corps de ballet*, but also was a fine example of the Russian nineteenth-century style from which so much of The Royal Ballet's traditions are derived. Later, during Ashton's time, Nureyev also produced *The Nutcracker* for the Covent Garden company.

Ashton, therefore, did not keep all the choreographic opportunities for himself. In 1964 *Serenade* was mounted by the founder of the American style of classical ballet, George Balanchine. Two years later Balanchine's first important creation, *Apollo*, for the Diaghilev company in 1928, entered The Royal Ballet repertory. *Apollo* is an example of what is called neo-classical ballet and belongs to the period of strong French influence during the Diaghilev company's later years. But the supreme example of neo-classical choreography married to French period style of the 1920s came with Bronislava Nijinska's *Les Biches*.

Nijinska, sister of the great dancer Nijinsky, created this work originally in 1924 and it caught perfectly the French *chic* and elegance of its time. It made also great demands upon the dancers, technically and as actors, so that it was an immensely valuable, as well as historically important, addition to the British dance scene. Indeed this ballet and *Les Noces*, which Nijinska reproduced for The Royal Ballet in 1966, are, says Alexander Bland, 'the most distinctive contributions of Ashton's directorship'.[1]

Other famous choreographers whom Ashton brought from abroad were the Englishman Antony Tudor, long resident in the United States of America and like Ashton himself one of Rambert's first great choreographers, and the South African John Cranko, who had gone to direct the Stuttgart Ballet in Germany. Tudor produced one of his best-known works, *Lilac Garden*, first seen in 1936, but created also a new work, *Shadowplay*, in which Anthony Dowell showed an unusual side to his talent as the Boy with Matted Hair. John Cranko's most popular addition to the repertory at this time was *Card Game*, a good example of something rather rare, a comic ballet.

Notwithstanding this enrichment from outside Britain, the most important work continued to come from within Britain, from Ashton himself, and from Kenneth MacMillan. The fourth significant feature of Ashton's directorship, therefore, was the emergence of MacMillan as Ashton's obvious choreographic successor.

Ashton's own creations in these years included two of his best ballets, *The Dream* and *Enigma Variations*, both further emphasising the qualities of the new British school of classical ballet which he has helped so much to establish.

Stephen Jefferies as the Joker in Card Game, *30 October 1973. Music by Igor Stravinsky, choreography by John Cranko, designs by Dorothée Zippel. This comic ballet by Cranko was created for the Stuttgart Ballet in 1965 and taken into the repertory of the Royal Ballet Touring Company in 1973. Photo: Anthony Crickmay.*

MacMillan's creations of this time include *Romeo and Juliet, Song of the Earth* and *Concerto,* all ballets of high quality which confirmed him as a choreographer of international status. It seemed natural, therefore, that MacMillan should succeed Ashton on his retirement in the summer of 1970. Peter Wright soon joined MacMillan as associate director, responsible particularly for what was called the New Group, a much-reduced touring section of The Royal Ballet.

New developments under the direction of Kenneth MacMillan 1970–77, and Norman Morrice, 1977–

Ashton's retirement marked not only the departure of the first generation of The Royal Ballet, its founders, but also a change in the structure which de Valois had created. The touring company and the Covent Garden company were merged and a small new group which was to be much more experimental than the big touring company could afford to be, was formed. This experiment was not successful. The reasons why it did not work are given later in this chapter.

Meanwhile, the arrival of a new style as well as a new director was signalled in MacMillan's first major production of his directorship, *Anastasia*. Produced in 1971, *Anastasia* is a three-act ballet which is part dance narrative in Act One, telling the story of the last years of the family of Tsar Nicholas II, part traditional classical spectacle in the Court dances of Act Two, and part a development of MacMillan's style of psychological dance-drama in Act Three. This exemplifies the blending of classicism and modern dance movements which subsequently MacMillan evolved most distinctly in *Manon, Mayerling* and *Isadora*.

This new choreographic direction was developed alongside new productions of the nineteenth and early twentieth century classics under both MacMillan and his successor Norman Morrice. MacMillan resigned as Director of The Royal Ballet in 1977, in order to concentrate on choreography, and is now principal choreographer to The Royal Ballet. He was succeeded by Norman Morrice former Director of Ballet Rambert. It might be useful to examine the thirteen years 1970–83, as a whole in order to appreciate the complementary aims of the two directors and to determine some shifts in emphasis that each has introduced.

MacMillan's contributions as director included an increased encouragement of choreographers from the United States of America, the introduction of the Russian dancers Natalia Makarova and Mikhail Baryshnikov to supplement the influence of Nureyev, the encouragement of young dancers, and a continuation but redefinition of the company's classical inheritance.

Norman Morrice's first objective on becoming Director of The Royal Ballet was to increase the number of performances given by young dancers. This he achieved by a temporary ban on guest artists which allowed greater opportunities for dancers to perform a wider variety of roles and achieve more speedy promotion within the company. This and his continuing policy of reassessing the classics have been some of the hallmarks of his period as director so far. It might be beneficial to look at some of the above points in greater detail.

American choreographers at Covent Garden

The two American choreographers whose works were new to Covent Garden at this time were Jerome Robbins and Glen Tetley, and their ballets now entered the repertory alongside further works by the master of American classical ballet, George Balanchine.

George Balanchine
De Valois and Ashton had both introduced some of his ballets into the repertory of The Royal Ballet and three more, *The Prodigal Son, The Four Temperaments* and *Agon*, were brought into the repertory in 1973. *The Prodigal Son* belongs to Balanchine's early period when he launched his career as a choreographer working for Diaghilev. *The Four Temperaments*, produced first in New York in 1946, belongs to a later time when not only Balanchine, but also his company, New York City Ballet and its school, had become the accepted centre of classical ballet in the United States of America. *Agon* illustrates also Balanchine's long and close association with the great composer Stravinsky: MacMillan himself choreographed a version of *Agon* in 1958, a year after New York City Ballet's première of Balanchine's ballet. In 1979 Norman Morrice added *Liebeslieder Walzer*, and in 1982 a revised version of *Apollo*.

Jerome Robbins
Jerome Robbins, choreographer of the famous musical drama *West Side Story*, had not worked with The Royal Ballet until the 1970s. MacMillan introduced five of Robbins' ballets at roughly annual intervals beginning with *Dances at a Gathering* in 1970. This was followed by *Afternoon of a Faun* in 1971, *Requiem Canticles* in 1972, *In the Night* in 1973 and *The Concert* in 1975. All of these ballets, albeit relatively small-cast, added valuable experience and challenges not only to the British dancers but also to the taste of British audiences.

Glen Tetley
The biggest challenge to established taste however came from Glen

Tetley, who produced *Field Figures* for the company in 1971 and *Laborintus* in 1972. Although based on classical techniques these two ballets were much more modern in both their style of music and choreography than had been seen before at the Royal Opera House. The score of taped sound effects for *Field Figures* was by the German composer Stockhausen and the equally difficult score for *Laborintus* was by the Italian, Luciano Berio. The experiment ably demonstrated that the dancers could master such a new style within their classical training. Tetley produced his *Voluntaries* for the company in 1976 and *Dances of Albion* in 1980, both more recognisably classical works.

Redefinition of the company's classical inheritance

MacMillan's redefinition of the company's classical inheritance came about in three ways. First was his introduction of classical choreographers, especially the Americans, whose work reflected strong modern influence. Second was a rethinking of traditional classical ballets. In February 1971 he introduced a revised Touring Company production of *Swan Lake* followed in March 1971 by Peter Wright's carefully thought-out production of *Giselle*, also a former Touring Company production. This was followed two years later by a version of *The Sleeping Beauty*.

Norman Morrice has continued this policy of reassessing the classics through new productions. The first new production of his directorship was a version of *The Sleeping Beauty* at Covent Garden, supervised by Dame Ninette de Valois. He has subsequently introduced new productions of *Swan Lake* and *Giselle*.

But the most important development of the classical inheritance lies in MacMillan's own contribution as choreographer and there has been a steady stream of new works by him throughout this thirteen-year period. Besides his large-scale ballets already mentioned, he recaptured with great subtlety the mood of the 1920s and 1930s respectively in *Elite Syncopations* and *La Fin du jour*. In 1980 he created an extraordinarily moving evocation of the First World War in *Gloria*, followed soon after by a production of *My Brother, My Sisters*, an intensely tortured study of family relationships created two years earlier for the Stuttgart Ballet.

Today it can be said with assurance that The Royal Ballet has in MacMillan a choreographer of world stature. More than this, there are a number of young choreographers following his example, and strongly encouraged by Norman Morrice, displaying their talents at the Royal Opera House. David Bintley created his first ballet for Covent Garden, *Adieu*, in 1980 and two of Michael Corder's ballets have received premières there, *L'Invitation au voyage* and *The White Goddess* (the latter for the Royal Ballet School). We shall return briefly to this future after a glance at The Royal Ballet's other important contribution to British dance: its relationship with audiences outside London.

Sadler's Wells Royal Ballet 1946–

The beginning of the second of the two Royal Ballet companies dates from the time Sadler's Wells Ballet moved to the Royal Opera House, Covent Garden, in 1946.

Sadler's Wells Opera continued to need dancers for its operas and Sadler's Wells Ballet recognised its own need for a company where dancers and choreographers could be developed. In any case, the connection with Sadler's Wells Theatre was by then too strong to be lightly thrown away. Sadler's Wells Ballet also had acquired obligations during the war to audiences throughout Britain. It was no longer a London company but a national company. A second company therefore was established at Sadler's Wells Theatre in 1946. First known as Sadler's Wells Opera Ballet, its name was changed in 1947 to Sadler's Wells Theatre Ballet. Ninette de Valois was its director as well as director of the larger company at the Royal Opera House. However, the main creative influence upon the new company was that of Peggy van Praagh, at first its ballet mistress, then assistant director under de Valois.

For ten years, from 1946 to 1956, this company was a nursery of talent. John Cranko, Kenneth MacMillan, and Peter Darrell, all future choreographers, were amongst its original dancers, but it developed also a style of its own and presented ballets by established choreographers like Ashton and Andrée Howard, whose finest ballet, *La Fête étrange* is still in the British repertory.

The company presented two or three performances a week at Sadler's Wells Theatre, alternating with the opera company, but also went on regional tours of many weeks, thus introducing The Royal Ballet's permanent presence to the British regions. At the same time, this combination of regular London and regional performances developed the company's potential as a training ground for dancers as well as choreographers. Svetlana Beriosova, Elaine Fifield, Nadia Nerina, Maryon Lane, Anne Heaton, David Poole, David Blair and Stanley Holden were early members who subsequently became well-known dancers.

Thus Sadler's Wells Theatre Ballet made a very important creative contribution to the future repertory and standards of The Royal Ballet. John Cranko and Kenneth MacMillan both created their earliest choreography for it. Cranko's *Pineapple Poll* and *The Lady and the Fool* remain in British repertory today, as does MacMillan's *Danses Concertantes* and *Solitaire*. Besides this, the company presented to its regional audiences, and on foreign tours to North

America, Europe and South Africa, small-scale productions of classical ballets like *Coppélia*, *The Nutcracker* and *Swan Lake*. It played, too, an important part in reviving parts of the company's British heritage, such as de Valois' *The Rake's Progress*, which were better suited to smaller stages than to the Royal Opera House.

By 1955, however, it was becoming more and more difficult for the company at Covent Garden to tour the regions because of its size and other commitments. Better to serve the regions, therefore, Sadler's Wells Theatre Ballet was gradually enlarged from about thirty to sixty dancers, and John Field took over from Peggy van Praagh as director.

The new size meant that the classics could be mounted in a more satisfactory style. Leading dancers from Covent Garden were to be guest artists with the touring company, supplementing its own principal dancers. Before long, The Royal Ballet's 'touring company', as it came to be known, had established itself so well in the affections of its regional public that its leading dancers like Doreen Wells and David Wall were as well known as some of the names from Covent Garden.

The company continued also its role as developer of choreographers. Kenneth MacMillan took over from John Cranko as resident choreographer and created a succession of new works, two of which, *The Burrow* and *The Invitation*, introduced dance-dramas of psychological conflict, an interest which MacMillan is still developing today.

The new size meant that some of Frederick Ashton's larger ballets could be introduced to regional audiences, for example *La Fille mal gardée*, his comic classic, and *The Dream*, his dance interpretation of Shakespeare's *A Midsummer Night's Dream*. Additionally, Ashton created original ballets for the company, such as *The Two Pigeons* and *Sinfonietta*. In the summer of 1964 the company became the vehicle through which Nureyev was able to mount his first production of Petipa's three-act ballet, *Raymonda*.

But it was mainly for its extensive touring in Britain and abroad and for its productions of the big classical ballets, including *The Sleeping Beauty*, that the company came to be known, winning an ever-growing public not only in Britain but also in Europe. This company was disbanded in the summer of 1970 largely because it was felt that it duplicated The Royal Ballet at Covent Garden and that the financial burden of maintaining such a large touring section was too great.

The New Group, as it was known, under the direction of Peter

Lynn Seymour as the Girl and Desmond Kelly as the Husband in a revival of The Invitation. First produced by the Touring Company on 10 November 1960, this is one of Kenneth MacMillan's tense psychological ballets. Music by Matyas Seiber, designs by Nicholas Georgiadis.
Photo: Anthony Crickmay.

Wright, aimed to provide a place for experimental work whilst keeping alive also a Royal Ballet presence in the regions. However, there were considerable problems. The tradition of The Royal Ballet's classical productions in the regions was too strong to be replaced with new experimental ideas. Audiences fell. Consequently, by 1973 the company was restored to approximately fifty dancers with a modified repertory, including established ballets like Ashton's *Les Patineurs* and de Valois' *The Rake's Progress*, alongside the pioneer choreography of the previous two years, like Glen Tetley's *Field Figures*, specially created for the New Group, and a piece by MacMillan called *Checkpoint*, in which two dancers crawled across walls covered with stretch material. This restoration began to recapture the lost audiences. *Giselle* and *Coppélia* were both produced by Peter Wright who had become an increasingly influential force in his own right in The Royal Ballet's hierarchy.

Finally, at a Gala performance at Sadler's Wells Theatre in September 1976, a change of name confirmed the end of the concept of the New Group as an experimental outpost of the company at Covent Garden. The New Group became Sadler's Wells Royal Ballet, based at Sadler's Wells Theatre.

Increasingly since then, Sadler's Wells Royal Ballet has developed an independent character and reputation, although it still reflects the twin tasks of the New Group, which were to take The Royal Ballet to the regions and to introduce new works. Today however, these tasks are now in better balance. Consequently the repertory can include a daringly experimental psychological dance-drama like MacMillan's *Playground*, alongside a production by Galina Samsova of the grand *pas* from Petipa's *Paquita*, a pure statement of classical tradition. In 1981, Samsova's value as communicator and interpreter of classical tradition was confirmed through a critically acclaimed version of *Swan Lake* by herself and Peter Wright.

The mix then, is exciting and stimulating for dancers and audiences alike and is winning increasing recognition abroad through successful foreign as well as British tours. Essentially, in Alexander Bland's phrase, Sadler's Wells Royal Ballet today 'is an improved and enlarged version'[2] of the Sadler's Wells Theatre Ballet of 1946, because it retains its role as a nursery of choreographic talent alongside its presentation of the classics and works from The Royal Ballet's repertory.

Not since the days of the Theatre Ballet when John Cranko and Kenneth MacMillan were both beginners, has The Royal Ballet been so rich in choreographic promise. Sadler's Wells Royal Ballet has provided first professional opportunities to David Bintley, Jonathan Burrows and Michael Corder. As previously mentioned, both Bintley and Corder have since choreographed works for The Royal Ballet at Covent Garden. This choreographic interdependence of the two companies, together with their sharing of repertory and their nurturing of native talent both for dancing and choreography, underlines their common aims. Both The Royal Ballet and Sadler's Wells Royal Ballet can be seen as exponents of the English style of classical ballet, as the preservers of the rich and

Galina Samsova as Odette and David Ashmole as Prince Siegfried in Swan Lake, *27 November 1981. Music by Tchaikovsky, choreography by Peter Wright, produced by Galina Samsova and Peter Wright, designs by Philip Prowse.*
Photo: Leslie E. Spatt.

varied inheritance of classical ballet with the ability at the same time to assimilate and profit from contact with modern dance idioms.

References

1. Bland, A. (1981) *The Royal Ballet: The first 50 years.* London: Threshold Books.
2. *Ibid.*

Suggested Further Reading

Brinson, P. and Crisp, C. (1981) *A guide to repertory: ballet and dance*. London: David and Charles.

* Clarke, M. (1955) *The Sadler's Wells Ballet*. London: A. & C. Black.

De Valois, N. (1981) *Come dance with me*. London: Dance Books.

Newman, B. and Spatt, L.E. (1983) *Sadler's Wells Royal Ballet Swan Lake*. London: Dance Books.

Percival, J. (1979) *The facts about a ballet company: featuring Sadler's Wells Royal Ballet*. London: G. Whizzard Publications.

Streatfield, N. (1959) *The Royal Ballet School*. London: Collins.

Thorpe, E. (1981) *Creating a ballet: MacMillan's Isadora*. London: Evans Brothers.

* White, F. (1951) *Sadler's Wells Ballet goes abroad*. London: Faber and Faber.

* Now out of print but well worth searching for in second-hand book-shops and your local library.

The Royal Ballet and Sadler's Wells Royal Ballet Chart

1926
Ninette de Valois opens the Academy of
Choreographic Art and is employed by
Lilian Baylis to provide ballets in operas
at the Old Vic.

1931
5 May 1931, first full evening of ballets
by the Vic-Wells Ballet, director Ninette
de Valois, at the Old Vic.
Academy of Choreographic Art
renamed the Vic-Wells Ballet School.

1941
Vic-Wells Ballet becomes Sadler's Wells
Ballet.

Sadler's Wells Ballet becomes resident ballet company at the Royal Opera House.	**1946**	Smaller company, Sadler's Wells Opera Ballet, formed at Sadler's Wells Theatre. Ballet mistress: Peggy van Praagh.
	1947	Sadler's Wells Opera Ballet becomes Sadler's Wells Theatre Ballet. Director: Peggy van Praagh.
Sadler's Wells Ballet's first tour to the United States of America.	**1949**	
	1956	John Field succeeds Peggy van Praagh as director of Sadler's Wells Theatre Ballet.

Company receives Royal Charter.

Sadler's Wells Ballet becomes The Royal Ballet; school becomes the Royal Ballet School.		Sadler's Wells Theatre Ballet becomes The Royal Ballet Touring Company.
Frederick Ashton succeeds Ninette de Valois as director.	**1963**	
Kenneth MacMillan succeeds Frederick Ashton as director, with Peter Wright as associate director.	**1970**	Touring Company becomes the New Group. Director: Peter Wright.
	1976	New Group becomes Sadler's Wells Royal Ballet. Director: Peter Wright.
Norman Morrice succeeds Kenneth MacMillan as director.	**1977**	

1981
The Royal Ballet celebrates its fiftieth
anniversary.

The Royal Ballet and Sadler's Wells Royal Ballet: chorechronicle of works mentioned in the chapter 1. All ballets in the repertory of the Vic-Wells, Sadler's Wells and The Royal Ballet mentioned in the text.

DATE OF FIRST PERFORMANCE BY THE ROYAL BALLET	TITLE	CHOREOGRAPHER	COMPOSER	DESIGNER	DATE OF FIRST PERFORMANCE IF ORIGINALLY PRODUCED ELSEWHERE
1931	Job	de Valois	Vaughan Williams	Gwendolen Raverat (after William Blake and Hedley Briggs)	1931 Camargo Society, London
1932	Les Sylphides	Fokine	Chopin	Bakst	First performed under the title *Les Sylphides* by Diaghilev's Ballets Russes, 1909
1933	Les Rendezvous	Ashton	Auber arr. Lambert	William Chappell	
1934	Giselle	after Coralli (Sergeyev)	Adam	Barbara Allen and William Chappell	1841, Paris Opéra
1934	Swan Lake	Petipa and Ivanov (Sergeyev)	Tchaikovsky	Hugh Stevenson	1895, Imperial Russian Ballet, St. Petersburg
1934	The Nutcracker	Ivanov and Petipa (Sergeyev)	Tchaikovsky	Hedley Briggs	1892, Imperial Russian Ballet, St. Petersburg
1935	The Rake's Progress	de Valois	Gavin Gordon	Rex Whistler after Hogarth	
1935	Façade	Ashton	Walton	John Armstrong	1931, Camargo Society, London
1936	Apparitions	Ashton	Liszt arr. Lambert	Cecil Beaton	
1937	Les Patineurs	Ashton	Meyerbeer arr. Lambert	William Chappell	
1937	Checkmate	de Valois	Arthur Bliss	E. McKnight Kauffer	
1939	The Sleeping Princess	Petipa (Sergeyev)	Tchaikovsky	Nadia Benois	1890, Imperial Russian Ballet, Maryinsky Theatre, St. Petersburg
1942	Hamlet	Helpmann	Tchaikovsky	Leslie Hurry	
1942	Comus	Helpmann	Purcell arr. Lambert	Oliver Messel	

DATE OF FIRST PERFORMANCE BY THE ROYAL BALLET	TITLE	CHOREOGRAPHER	COMPOSER	DESIGNER	DATE OF FIRST PERFORMANCE IF ORIGINALLY PRODUCED ELSEWHERE
1944	Miracle in the Gorbals	Helpmann	Arthur Bliss	Edward Burra	
1946	Adam Zero	Helpmann	Arthur Bliss	Roger Furse	
1946	Symphonic Variations	Ashton	César Franck	Sophie Fedorovitch	
1946	The Sleeping Beauty	after Petipa (Sergeyev)	Tchaikovsky	Oliver Messel	1890, Imperial Russian Ballet, St. Petersburg
1947	The Three-Cornered Hat	Massine	de Falla	Picasso	1919, Diaghilev's Ballets Russes, London
1948	Cinderella	Ashton	Prokofiev	Jean-Denis Malclès	
1950	Ballet Imperial	Balanchine	Tchaikovsky	Eugene Berman	1941, American Ballet Caravan, New York
1954	The Firebird	Fokine	Stravinsky	Natalia Goncharova	1910, Diaghilev's Ballets Russes, Paris
1955	The Lady and the Fool	Cranko	Verdi arr. Mackerras	Richard Beer	1954, Sadler's Wells Theatre Ballet, Oxford
1958	Agon	MacMillan	Stravinsky	Nicholas Georgiadis	
1959	Danses Concertantes	MacMillan	Stravinsky	Nicholas Georgiadis	1955, Sadler's Wells Theatre Ballet, Sadler's Wells Theatre
1960	La Fille mal gardée	Ashton	Hérold and Lanchbery	Osbert Lancaster	
1962	The Rite of Spring	MacMillan	Stravinsky,	Sydney Nolan	1960, Royal Ballet Touring Company, Oxford
1962	The Invitation	MacMillan	Matyas Seiber	Nicholas Georgiadis	
1962	Flower Festival at Genzano	Bournonville	E. Helsted	Richard Beer	1858, Royal Danish Ballet, Copenhagen
1962	Napoli pas-de-six	Bournonville	E. Helsted and Paulli	Richard Beer	1842, Royal Danish Ballet, Copenhagen
1963	La Bayadère	Petipa (Nureyev)	Minkus	Philip Prowse	1877, Imperial Russian Ballet, St. Petersburg
1964	Serenade	Balanchine	Tchaikovsky		1934, School of American Ballet, New York
1964	The Dream	Ashton	Mendelssohn arr. Lanchbery	Henry Bardon and David Walker	

1964	Les Biches	Nijinska	Poulenc	Marie Laurençin	1924, Diaghilev's Ballets Russes, Monte Carlo
1965	Romeo and Juliet	MacMillan	Prokofiev	Nicholas Georgiadis	
1966	Apollo	Balanchine	Stravinsky	John Craxton	1928, Diaghilev's Ballets Russes, Paris
1966	Les Noces	Nijinska	Stravinsky	Natalia Goncharova	1923, Diaghilev's Ballets Russes, Paris
1966	Card Game	Cranko	Stravinsky	Dorothée Zippel	1965, the Stuttgart Ballet, Stuttgart
1966	Song of the Earth	MacMillan	Mahler	Nicholas Georgiadis	1965, the Stuttgart Ballet, Stuttgart
1967	Shadowplay	Tudor	Charles Koechlin	Michael Annals	
1968	The Nutcracker	Nureyev	Tchaikovsky	Nicholas Georgiadis	1892, Imperial Russian Ballet, St. Petersburg
1968	Lilac Garden	Tudor	Chausson	Lingwood and Stevenson	1936, Ballet Rambert, London
1968	Enigma Variations	Ashton	Elgar	Julia Trevelyan-Oman	
1970	Concerto	MacMillan	Shostakovich	Jürgen Rose	1966, German Opera Ballet, Berlin
1970	Dances at a Gathering	Robbins	Chopin	Joe Eula	1969, New York City Ballet, New York
1971	Swan Lake	Petipa, Ivanov, and others (Sergeyev)	Tchaikovsky	Leslie Hurry	1895, Imperial Russian Ballet, St. Petersburg
1971	Giselle	Coralli and Perrot (Peter Wright)	Adam	Peter Farmer	1841, Paris Opéra
1971	Anastasia	MacMillan	Tchaikovsky, Martinů and STU West Berlin	Barry Kay	
1971	Afternoon of a Faun	Robbins	Debussy	Jean Rosenthal and Irene Sharaff	1953, New York City Ballet, New York
1971	Field Figures	Tetley	Stockhausen	Nadine Baylis	1970, Royal Ballet New Group, Nottingham
1972	Laborintus	Tetley	Berio	Rouben Ter-Arutunian	
1972	Requiem Canticles	Robbins	Stravinsky		1972, New York City Ballet, New York
1973	In the Night	Robbins	Chopin	Anthony Dowell	1970, New York City Ballet, New York

DATE OF FIRST PERFORMANCE BY THE ROYAL BALLET	TITLE	CHOREOGRAPHER	COMPOSER	DESIGNER	DATE OF FIRST PERFORMANCE IF ORIGINALLY PRODUCED ELSEWHERE
1973	The Prodigal Son	Balanchine	Prokofiev	Georges Rouault	1929, Diaghilev's Ballets Russes, Paris
1973	Agon	Balanchine	Stravinsky		1957, New York City Ballet, New York
1973	The Four Temperaments	Balanchine	Hindemith		1946, Ballet Society, New York
1974	Manon	MacMillan	Massenet	Nicholas Georgiadis	
1974	Elite Syncopations	MacMillan	Scott Joplin and others	Ian Spurling	
1975	The Concert	Robbins	Chopin	Irene Sharaff	1956, New York City Ballet, New York
1976	Voluntaries	Tetley	Poulenc	Rouben Ter-Arutunian	1973, the Stuttgart Ballet, Stuttgart
1977	The Sleeping Beauty	Petipa, after Sergeyev, and Ashton (de Valois)	Tchaikovsky	David Walker	1890, Imperial Russian Ballet, St. Petersburg
1978	Mayerling	MacMillan	Liszt arr. Lanchbery	Nicholas Georgiadis	
1979	Swan Lake	Petipa, Ivanov and others (Norman Morrice)	Tchaikovsky	Leslie Hurry	1895, Imperial Russian Ballet, St. Petersburg
1979	La Fin du jour	MacMillan	Ravel	Ian Spurling	
1979	Liebeslieder Walzer	Balanchine	Brahms	David Hays and Karinska	1960, New York City Ballet, New York
1980	Gloria	MacMillan	Poulenc	Andy Klunder	
1980	Giselle	Coralli and Perrot, rev. Sergeyev, Ashton (Norman Morrice)	Adam	James Bailey	1841, Paris Opéra
1980	My Brother, My Sisters	MacMillan	Schoenberg and Webern	Yolanda Sonnabend	1978, the Stuttgart Ballet, Stuttgart
1980	Adieu	Bintley	Panufnik	Mike Becket	
1980	Dances of Albion	Tetley	Britten	Santo Loquasto	
1981	Isadora	MacMillan	Rodney Bennett	Barry Kay	
1982	L'Invitation au voyage	Corder	Duparc	Yolanda Sonnabend	

2. All ballets in the repertory of the Sadler's Wells Theatre Ballet, Royal Ballet Touring Company, New Group and Sadler's Wells Royal Ballet referred to by title in text.

DATE OF FIRST PERFORMANCE BY SADLER'S WELLS ROYAL BALLET	TITLE	CHOREOGRAPHER	COMPOSER	DESIGNER	DATE OF FIRST PERFORMANCE IF ORIGINALLY PRODUCED ELSEWHERE
1947	Le Féte étrange	Andrée Howard	Fauré	Sophie Fedorovitch	1940, London Ballet, London
1948	Capriol Suite	Ashton	Peter Warlock	William Chappell	1930, Rambert Dancers, London
1949	Beauty and the Beast	Cranko	Ravel	Margaret Kaye	
1951	The Nutcracker	Ivanov arr. Ashton	Tchaikovsky	Cecil Beaton	1892, Imperial Russian Ballet, St. Petersburg
1951	Pineapple Poll	Cranko	Sullivan arr. Mackerras	Osbert Lancaster	
1951	Coppélia	Ivanov and Cecchetti (Sergeyev)	Delibes	Loudon Sainthill	Original production by Saint-Léon, Paris Opera, 1870; Petipa/Ivanov version, St. Petersburg, 1884
1952	The Rake's Progress	de Valois	Gavin Gordon	Rex Whistler after Hogarth	1935, Vic-Wells Ballet at Sadler's Wells Theatre
1954	The Lady and the Fool	Cranko	Verdi arr. Mackerras	Richard Beer	
1955	Danses Concertantes	MacMillan	Stravinsky	Nicholas Georgiadis	
1955	Les Patineurs	Ashton	Meyerbeer arr. Lambert	William Chappell	1937, Vic-Wells Ballet at Sadler's Wells Theatre
1956	Solitaire	MacMillan	Malcolm Arnold	Desmond Heeley	
1958	The Burrow	MacMillan	Frank Martin	Nicholas Georgiadis	
1958	Swan Lake	Petipa, Ivanov and Ashton after Petipa (Sergeyev)	Tchaikovsky	Leslie Hurry	1895, Imperial Russian Ballet, St. Petersburg
1959	The Sleeping Beauty		Tchaikovsky	Oliver Messel	
1960	The Invitation	MacMillan	Matyas Seiber	Nicholas Georgiadis	
1961	The Two Pigeons	Ashton	Messager	Jacques Dupont	

DATE OF FIRST PERFORMANCE BY SADLER'S WELLS ROYAL BALLET	TITLE	CHOREOGRAPHER	COMPOSER	DESIGNER	DATE OF FIRST PERFORMANCE IF ORIGINALLY PRODUCED ELSEWHERE
1962	La Fille mal gardée	Ashton	Hérold arr. Lanchbery	Osbert Lancaster	1960, The Royal Ballet at the Royal Opera House
1964	Raymonda	Nureyev after Petipa	Glazunov	Beni Montresor	1898, Maryinsky Theatre, St. Petersburg
1966	Raymonda Act III	Nureyev after Petipa	Glazunov	Barry Kay	1898, Maryinsky Theatre, St. Petersburg
1966	The Dream	Ashton	Mendelssohn arr. Lanchbery	Peter Farmer	1964, The Royal Ballet at the Royal Opera House
1967	Sinfonietta	Ashton	Malcolm Williamson	Peter Rice	
1968	Giselle	Petipa after Coralli/ Perrot, revised Sergeyev (Peter Wright)	Adam	Peter Farmer	
1970	Checkpoint	MacMillan	Roberto Gerhard	Elisabeth Dalton	
1970 1975	Field Figures Coppélia	Tetley after Petipa and Cecchetti, Peter Wright (P. Wright)	Stockhausen Delibes	Nadine Baylis Osbert Lancaster	Original production by Saint-Léon, Paris Opéra, 1870; Petipa/Ivanov version St. Petersburg,1884
1979	Playground	MacMillan	Gordon Crosse	Yolanda Sonnabend	
1980	Paquita	Petipa (Samsova)	Minkus	Peter Farmer	1881, Bolshoi Theatre, St. Petersburg
1981	Swan Lake	Petipa, Samsova and Wright (Samsova and Wright)	Tchaikovsky	Philip Prowse	1895, Imperial Russian Ballet, St. Petersburg

Chapter 3

London Festival Ballet

Claire Teverson

The history of London Festival Ballet can be divided into four
major sections:

1949–64	the founding of the company by Dr Julian Braunsweg, Anton Dolin and Alicia Markova, and its early years first as a touring company and later as a company of international repute,
1965–68	London Festival Ballet under the direction of Donald Albery,
1968–79	Beryl Grey as artistic director,
1979–	The directorship of John Field and the way ahead.

These four sections are discussed in this chapter under the head-
ings of:

> personalities
> policies
> achievements.

1949–64: The founding of Festival Ballet and its early years

Personalities

Dr Julian Braunsweg

London Festival Ballet was formed in 1950. It was the inspiration primarily of Dr Julian Braunsweg, a skilful impresario who had previously promoted tours in Europe for Anna Pavlova and Colonel de Basil's Ballets Russes. Dr Braunsweg recognised that the time was ripe to develop a new company as during the Second World War the interest in the arts and particularly dance had increased. He realised that to achieve recognition he would require well-known artists and artistic directors, so he turned to the internationally famous Anton Dolin and Alicia Markova. The only major companies at this time in London were the Sadler's Wells Company and Ballet Rambert. Both Braunsweg and Dolin were determined to take classical ballet to a wider audience.

Anton Dolin

The choice of Anton Dolin as principal dancer and artistic director gave the company a British star already well-established internationally.

Anton Dolin was born in 1904 in Sussex. His real name was Patrick Healey-Kay. His father was English and his mother Irish. He attended the famous Italia Conti school and as a child he appeared in many theatrical productions. His main interest at that time was in becoming a dancer, and in 1917 his mother took him to meet the great Russian teacher, Seraphina Astafieva. Astafieva encouraged his dancing ambitions and gave him the tuition he needed. When Diaghilev came to Astafieva's dancing academy in 1921 he picked out this promising pupil whom he called Patrikieff and gave him some minor roles in his company's production of *The Sleeping Princess*, the ballet now known as *The Sleeping Beauty*.

Two years later Healey-Kay joined Diaghilev's company, the Ballets Russes, and on 1 January 1924 he danced his first leading role with the company in Monte Carlo. It was the first time that an Englishman had ever danced a principal role in Diaghilev's ballet company. He had already changed his name to Anton Dolin, for to be taken seriously as a dancer, it was important to have a Russian name. Dolin danced with Diaghilev's company at various times over the next few years. He also continued to appear in theatrical revues which made him well-known to London audiences.

In 1934 he joined the Vic-Wells Ballet Company as principal dancer and partnered Alicia Markova in a production of *Giselle*. This partnership continued when in the following year they formed the Markova-Dolin Company and toured widely in Britain until 1938.

The following year Dolin went to Australia with Colonel de Basil's Ballets Russes and then on to America where he was closely involved with the American Ballet Theatre in its early days. There he worked not only as a principal dancer, but also as a choreographer. In 1941 he staged his version of the *Pas de Quatre* based on the original 1845 version by Jules Perrot.

In 1948 Dolin returned with Markova as guests of Sadler's Wells Ballet to dance many classical roles. Following this season in London, Dolin and Markova realised that there was a growing demand for popular classical ballet. However, many people were unable to travel to London to see performances, or even if they lived in the capital, they often could not afford tickets for Covent Garden. In January 1949, Dolin and Markova appeared at the huge Empress Hall, Earls Court, for six nights with a small group of dancers from the Cone-Ripman School of Dancing, later to become the Arts Educational School. In order to achieve success in this new venture, Dolin presented short ballets and well-known excerpts such as the solo of *The Dying Swan* and the *pas de deux* from *The Nutcracker*.

It was the success of this great partnership that led to Dr Braunsweg's proposal that Markova should also be a co-founder of the new company.

Alicia Markova

Alicia Markova was born in London in 1910. Her real name was Alicia Marks. As a child she was very frail and at the suggestion of a doctor, her mother took her to dancing lessons to strengthen her limbs. She attended a dancing academy and for several years performed in many shows. Her mother then took her to the studio of Seraphina Astafieva, where she had lessons along with her future partner, Anton Dolin.

At the age of fourteen she joined the Diaghilev company as the youngest dancer ever to be accepted and Diaghilev himself renamed her Alicia Markova. In 1929 she made her first appearance with Anton Dolin when they danced the Blue Bird *pas de deux* from the third act of *The Sleeping Beauty*.

After the death of Diaghilev in 1929, the company disbanded and Markova appeared in many performances with Marie Rambert's Ballet Club, particularly in works choreographed by Frederick Ashton. In 1932 she accepted Ninette de Valois' invitation and joined the Vic-Wells Ballet Company. There she was an enormous success and she became the first British dancer to appear as Giselle. Markova remained with the company as prima ballerina until 1935.

For the next two years Dolin partnered Markova in their own company (called the Markova-Dolin Ballet) and by the end of their tours together Markova had established herself as the first British ballerina of international repute. On many occasions over the next ten years Markova and Dolin danced together. She joined him with the Ballets Russes Company and later the American Ballet Theatre. She then returned to England for a series of provincial tours with Dr Braunsweg's newly formed company. In 1950, whilst recovering in hospital from an illness, Markova thought of a name for the company. She decided that as 1951 was the year of the Festival of Britain, the company should be called Festival Ballet.

Markova left the company in 1951, but she returned many times to dance with them as a guest artist.

John Gilpin

It is interesting to note that during Dr Braunsweg's era many young dancers achieved considerable personal success. One such person was John Gilpin who joined the company in 1950. He began his training at the Cone-Ripman School and then joined Ballet Rambert in 1945, where he became a principal dancer. At the age of twenty, he joined London Festival Ballet. As John Gilpin had had previous experience as a principal dancer, he was able to share many leading classical roles with Anton Dolin. One of his earliest leading roles with the company was in *Le Spectre de la Rose*, where he partnered Anita Landa who had also danced with the company from its early days.

Over the following years he partnered many internationally famous dancers. In 1956 he danced one of the principal roles in *Etudes* at the wedding of Prince Rainier and Princess Grace of Monaco. The televising of this ballet increased the recognition of

---

Co-founders of Festival Ballet: Alicia Markova and Anton Dolin in The Nutcracker *pas de deux, c. 1950.*
Photo: Houston Rogers. The Theatre Museum Crown Copyright.

John Gilpin, London Festival Ballet's leading dancer for many years in Etudes, 1966.
Photo: R.A.S. Barcelona.

the company as one of international repute. Many impresarios from this point insisted on Gilpin's presence when booking the company for foreign tours.

In 1960 he left London Festival Ballet along with Dolin and several other dancers. He returned as a dancer in the following year and was the company's artistic director from 1962 to 1965.

Policies

Throughout these early years, it was the policy of the company to tour and popularise ballet by using well-established dancers and choreographers. Initially the company consisted of a small *corps de ballet* from the Cone-Ripman School, with several soloists such as John Gilpin and, as the star attractions, Alicia Markova and Anton Dolin. Dolin planned a repertoire in which guest stars could appear, giving many people opportunities to see a number of internationally famous dancers. Alexandra Danilova, Yvette Chauviré, Tamara Toumanova, and Léonide Massine all danced with the company.

Both Dolin and Markova were classical dancers trained in the traditions of the Russian ballet. It was natural, therefore, that the company's repertoire included both the great classics like *Giselle* and *The Nutcracker*, and works from the Diaghilev repertoire. The ballet master and dancer, Nicholas Beriozoff, contributed a great deal to the success of the company, reviving works such as the Fokine ballets, *Petrouchka*, *Schéhérazade*, and *Prince Igor*.

Later on during this period as the company became more secure financially they were able to adopt a policy of introducing new works. Two ballets which are still in the company's repertoire are Harold Lander's *Etudes*, which was first performed by London Festival Ballet in 1955, and Jack Carter's *The Witch Boy*, first performed by the company in 1957. Two other works popular at this time were *Symphony for Fun* and *London Morning*, although these and many other new works were short-lived because the popularity of the company seemed to rest on the presentation of well-known classical ballets and international stars.

From the time of its formation the company toured the provinces, but Dr Braunsweg believed that in order to compete with the other two major British companies, it was important to establish a London season. This he successfully negotiated initially at the Stoll Theatre. The company's first season there was in October 1950 with a full-length production of *The Nutcracker* by Nicholas Beriozoff. Later the company also performed at the Royal Festival Hall, whilst continuing to present performances in the regions. He also felt it was necessary to make the company well known internationally. Previously Braunsweg had been connected with the Russian ballet, and as they had performed at the opera house at Monte Carlo, it was natural for him to turn to this as a suitable venue for London Festival Ballet. Following the establishment of a

The final scene of Petrouchka, *with Léonide Massine as Petrouchka, 1950.*
This was the first of several revivals for Festival Ballet.
Photo: Houston Rogers. The Theatre Museum Crown Copyright.

regular season in Monte Carlo, Dr Braunsweg pursued this policy of gaining fuller international recognition by arranging tours in numerous European countries and America.

Achievements

During this period the company gained the status of an international ballet company which was in demand overseas as well as in London and the regions. By 1953 they had established a pattern of overseas tours and annual seasons at the Royal Festival Hall.

One of Dr Braunsweg's greatest achievements for the company was the contract he made with the London County Council in 1952 for the Royal Festival Hall. This enabled them to present a Christmas and Summer season each year in London.

Perhaps the most popular production with family audiences proved to be *The Nutcracker*. The 1957 production was by David

Lichine with designs by Alexander Benois. The ballet still remains in the repertoire today although a number of changes to the story and choreography have been made.

As a result of increasing financial debts, caused in part by the expense of two productions by the Russian choreographer Vladimir Bourmeister of *The Snow Maiden* and *Swan Lake* (Act Two), Dr Braunsweg was forced to put the company into voluntary liquidation. In 1962, a non-profit making organisation was set up under the title of London Festival Ballet Enterprises Ltd. This meant that the company was now eligible for financial aid and the London County Council came to the rescue with a grant of £30,000.

In the final years of Dr Braunsweg's association with the company, one of the few new productions was a full-length ballet of *Peer Gynt* in 1963 by Vaslav Orlikowsky with music by Grieg. A new member of the company, Karl Musil, shared the leading role with John Gilpin. The company now had a strong collection of principal dancers including Galina Samsova, Irina Borowska, Lucette Aldous and André Prokovsky.

It was only the financial failure in 1965 of Orlikowsky's full-length production of *Swan Lake* that led to the end of Dr Braunsweg's directorship of the company of which he was so proud.

1965–68: London Festival Ballet under the direction of Donald Albery

Following the financial crisis of 1964–6, the Arts Council decided to intervene in order to safeguard the future of London Festival Ballet. Under the chairmanship of Lord Goodman, a trust was formed to plan the company's financial future. Donald Albery was appointed its director.

Donald Albery

Donald Albery had great experience in the theatrical world as he owned several West End theatres and had been manager of Sadler's Wells Ballet from 1941 to 1945.

A considerable grant was given by the Greater London Council and the Arts Council and Albery was allowed to administer the company's affairs with a fairly free hand. His first decision was to employ some of the dancers from the recently disbanded London Dance Theatre. This company had been founded by the dancer and designer Norman McDowell in 1964 and existed for only one year.

Jack Carter

Jack Carter, who had choreographed several ballets for London Dance Theatre was now appointed London Festival Ballet's first resident choreographer.

Policies

Donald Albery's immediate concern was to improve the company's financial position. He decided to commission the revival of popular classics, making use of existing sets and costumes. He therefore asked Jack Carter to produce new versions of *Swan Lake* and *The Nutcracker*.

After securing the company's finances, he pursued a policy of diversifying its repertoire. Some of his most interesting additions to the repertoire were Serge Lifar's *Noir et Blanc* and Balanchine's *Night Shadow*. In these and other productions it was Albery's policy to give some of the leading roles to the younger soloists within the company. He felt it was important that they should be given opportunities to dance alongside the company's principals and guest artists.

Albery provided opportunities for a variety of designers and technicians to work for the company. He invited two young designers, Peter Docherty and Peter Farmer, to create designs for several short works. Docherty and Farmer have continued their association with London Festival Ballet and have worked with other dance companies all over the world.

Achievements

During his three years as London Festival Ballet's director, Donald Albery saved the company from financial crisis and he managed to secure its future by placing it in a stronger financial position. The company has continued to receive regular grants from both the Arts Council and the Greater London Council.

The company's repertoire was also strengthened with the availability of more funds. Albery continued to commission the revival of the popular classics, including Jack Carter's new production of *Coppélia*.

The most important and ambitious production at this time was *The Sleeping Beauty*. It was produced by Ben Stevenson, who had previously danced with the company and had been one of the ballet masters. Norman McDowell designed the ballet and Beryl Grey was the artistic adviser. It was this elaborate production that provided many solos for the younger members of the company. For the première of *The Sleeping Beauty*, the French ballerina Noëlla Pontois was invited by Albery to dance with John Gilpin. Many of the later performances were danced by Galina Samsova and André Prokovsky, who were to lead the company over the next few years.

Albery continued to follow Dr Braunsweg's policy of touring both in the provincial towns and in numerous European countries. He successfully negotiated tours to Turkey and Japan, two countries which had not been visited by the company previously.

Towards the end of 1967 the Festival Ballet Trust was formed to supervise the company's finances and in 1968 Donald Albery resigned in order to devote time to his many other commitments.

1968–79: Beryl Grey as artistic director

After the resignation of Donald Albery, the governors of London Festival Ballet Trust decided that his position should be divided into two, giving the company an administrator and an artistic director. Wilfred Stiff was appointed administrator and Beryl Grey was appointed artistic director in May 1968.

Beryl Grey

Beryl Grey was born in London in 1927. Her real name was Beryl Groom. At the age of four she attended weekly dancing classes and by the age of nine she had passed all the Royal Academy of Dancing examinations. At the age of ten, Beryl Groom was awarded a scholarship by Ninette de Valois to attend the Vic-Wells Ballet School. She joined as the youngest pupil by two years in 1937.

She made her first appearance with the Sadler's Wells Company in 1941, when she danced in the *corps de ballet* in a production of *Giselle*. It was soon after this that Ninette de Valois gave her pupil the new name of Beryl Grey. When she was fourteen Beryl Grey was asked to replace Margot Fonteyn, who had been taken ill, in the role of Odette in *Swan Lake*. During the remainder of the war years she toured Britain with Sadler's Wells Ballet as a principal ballerina. She continued with the company until 1957 performing at Covent Garden, their new London home, and on tours in Europe, America and Canada. She also made many guest appearances during this time with foreign companies in cities such as Stockholm and Brussels.

In 1957 Beryl Grey resigned from The Royal Ballet and decided to become a free-lance ballerina. Having gained international recognition as a classical dancer, she became the first British ballerina to be invited to dance in the Soviet Union with the Bolshoi and Kirov Ballet Companies. Following this in 1964 she went to China to dance as a guest artist with the Peking National Ballet Company. As well as touring abroad she continued to dance in Britain, appearing with The Royal Ballet and London Festival Ballet.

In 1965 she made her final stage appearance in a gala with Ballet Rambert. She then became director general of the Arts Educational Schools.

In 1967 Donald Albery invited Beryl Grey, now a member of

London Festival Ballet's Board of Governors, to be the artistic adviser for the company's new production of *The Sleeping Beauty*. Her knowledge of this ballet was immense, having danced in many productions by different choreographers in the roles of the Lilac Fairy and Princess Aurora.

After her work on this new production Beryl Grey decided to resign from her post with the Arts Educational Trust and return to free-lance work, only this time as a teacher. When Donald Albery left London Festival Ballet, the chairman of the company's Board of Governors encouraged Beryl Grey to apply for the new post of artistic director. She was appointed to this position in May 1968.

Policies

When Beryl Grey took over the role of artistic director, she realised that there was an enormous challenge ahead of her. She brought to the company a sense of discipline and a great determination to improve artistic standards. Having spent much of her life with The Royal Ballet she was used to their formal and institutionalised approach to a dancer's training. London Festival Ballet had no training school, no permanent base or theatre, and therefore it was not surprising to her that their standards and approach were more informal than those at The Royal Ballet. The company had experienced a history of financial uncertainity and inevitably this had affected some of the dancers' attitudes to their career prospects within the company.

Beryl Grey recognised that London Festival Ballet had tremendous potential. Her immediate policy was to raise artistic standards and to instill into the company an overall unity of style and a more disciplined approach to performance. Some of the company found these changes were not to their liking. As a result Beryl Grey had to assert her authority by terminating several of the dancers' contracts. The majority of the company were behind her and her new policy, although for a period the fear of imminent dismissal prevailed throughout the company. As well as improving standards, Beryl Grey believed that the company needed more dancers. This was to ensure that when there were injuries or illness, the performance was not adversely affected. She also wanted to have in the company more principal dancers rather than relying on two or three artists to perform all the leading roles. It was her aim in time to promote dancers from within the company rather than engaging new principals from other companies.

It was also Beryl Grey's policy to extend the company's repertoire. She realised that it would always be necessary to perform the major classical productions as these provided a sound basis for the company and also much of its income. London Festival Ballet's regular audience was keen to attend lavish full-length productions with stories that were easily understood.

In 1971 Beryl Grey invited Mary Skeaping to stage a new version of *Giselle*. As well as adding to the number of full-length classical productions Beryl Grey wanted to diversify the repertoire still further by increasing the number of one-act ballets which had proved particularly successful when touring abroad. Her aim was to add to the number of works by particular choreographers who had been connected with the company previously.

Léonide Massine

She invited Léonide Massine to revive four of his ballets for the company: *Le Beau Danube* in 1971, *The Three-Cornered Hat* and *Gaîté Parisienne* in 1973, and *Parade* in 1974. Nicholas Beriozoff, the company's former ballet master, also returned to produce Fokine's *The Golden Cockerel* in 1976. This continued the company's tradition of reviving ballets created for the Ballets Russes.

Beryl Grey also believed that it was vitally important for the development of the company and the dancers to extend their range beyond the classical productions. However, for financial reasons the company was obliged to perform as frequently as possible and could not spare many weeks in the year for creating new ballets. Nevertheless Beryl Grey managed to a certain extent to pursue her policy of commissioning contemporary works by engaging Barry Moreland, a young choreographer trained in Graham technique, as the company's resident choreographer. He created *Summer Solstice* in 1972, *Prodigal Son (in Ragtime)* in 1974, and *Dancing Space* in 1976.

Each of these policies reflected Beryl Grey's overall aim to produce works that would give the company an image and a repertoire of its own.

When she joined London Festival Ballet, it was already well established as a touring company. It was Beryl Grey's policy to maintain these touring commitments but also to improve the international status of the company. She was determined to take the company on more prestigious foreign tours – performing for longer seasons at larger theatres. This she succeeded in doing when the company travelled to America, Australia and China.

Achievements

Beryl Grey remained with the London Festival Ballet as artistic director for eleven years and during that time the company developed and flourished under her direction. Her meticulous attention to detail and her constant striving for higher standards considerably enhanced the company's reputation both in Britain and abroad.

Perhaps the most important achievement during her first few years with the company was the acquisition of the London Coliseum for a regular Spring season. This gave London Festival Ballet an additional London season at a large theatre. The company still performs there today, as well as at the Royal Festival Hall.

It was the introduction of the Coliseum season that led to Beryl Grey increasing the range and number of works that the company were able to perform. She had to develop a repertoire that could do justice to the large London stages and also tour successfully without incurring enormous transportation costs for scenery and costumes. This she achieved, and in the last five years as artistic director she added a greater number of works to the repertoire than in any other similar period during the company's history. She succeeded in increasing the number of full-length classical ballets with lavish productions including Rudolf Nureyev's *The Sleeping Beauty* which was first performed by London Festival Ballet in 1975, the year of the company's twenty-fifth anniversary; *Romeo and Juliet* in 1977; Ronald Hynd's *The Nutcracker* in 1976 and *Rosalinda* in 1979; and Peter Schaufuss's *La Sylphide* in 1979.

Possibly Beryl Grey's greatest achievement in contributing to the repertoire was the engaging of Rudolf Nureyev to work with the company on his two full-length classical productions. The number of one-act ballets was also increased for the triple-bill presentations with works such as Antony Tudor's *Echoing of Trumpets* and Fokine's *Les Sylphides* produced by Alicia Markova in 1976. Another way in which Beryl Grey enlarged the repertoire was by the commissioning of contemporary pieces by Barry Moreland and guest choreographers such as Glen Tetley. Tetley staged his ballet *Greening* in 1978 and later *Sphinx* in 1979.

Gradually Beryl Grey managed to instill into the company a more disciplined approach. It soon became evident that the company was achieving a higher standard of performance and she was able to promote many of the dancers within the company to higher positions, for example, Alan Dubreuil and Dudley von

Paul Clarke and the Overture Ladies in Prodigal Son (in Ragtime), *1974.*
This popular ballet was set to the music of Scott Joplin.
Photo: Anthony Crickmay.

Loggenburg. Dancers from other companies came to join London
Festival Ballet. These included Maina Gielgud, and from The Royal
Ballet, Paul Clarke, Carole Hill and Patricia Ruanne.

In 1976 Beryl Grey achieved another of her dreams, the acquisition of a permanent home for the company. The Greater London
Council and the Arts Council of Great Britain gave financial assistance for the conversion of Queen Alexandra's House near the
Royal Albert Hall in London to rehearsal studios and company
headquarters. This gave the company a permanent base under one
roof and was given the new name of Festival Ballet House.

1979–: the directorship of John Field and the way ahead

Personalities

After eleven years as artistic director of London Festival Ballet, Beryl Grey left the company and was succeeded by John Field in November 1979. At the same time Elizabeth Anderton was appointed to the new position of assistant artistic director.

John Field

John Field was born in Yorkshire in 1921. He trained at the Elliott-Clarke school in Liverpool and joined the Vic-Wells Ballet Company in 1939. After the Second World War he returned to Sadler's Wells Ballet and became a principal dancer where he often partnered Beryl Grey. In 1956 he retired from performing and took over the direction of the Royal Ballet Touring Company. Here he achieved considerable success and in 1970 he was appointed joint director of The Royal Ballet with Kenneth MacMillan. In October 1971 he became artistic director of La Scala, Milan. John Field returned to this country and became director of the Royal Academy of Dancing in 1975 until joining London Festival Ballet in 1979.

Policies

John Field joined London Festival Ballet at a time when many companies and theatres were undergoing a period of great financial difficulty. Increased costs in presenting ballets, particularly when touring, made it very difficult for the company to keep within its budget. The visit to China in 1979 had been a great success artistically, but the enormous touring costs meant a financial loss was incurred. Other reasons for the company's deficit included a reduction in the number of people attending performances in London, and the government's increase in Value Added Tax on all theatre tickets.

It was therefore John Field's immediate policy to rationalise London Festival Ballet's repertoire but at the same time develop it by selecting ballets that were representative of the company. His aim was to maintain a balance of classical, romantic and contemporary works. For a time, the company had to concentrate on performing the most popular productions in the company's repertoire, for example, *Romeo and Juliet, Coppélia* and *Giselle* were performed for the 1981 London Coliseum season.

However, new short ballets were also created for the company: Barry Moreland returned in 1980 to choreograph *Journey to Avalon* and dancers Trevor Wood and Michael Pink also created works for the company.

A new policy introduced by John Field was to give more prominence to London Festival Ballet's own principals and to invite fewer guest artists to dance with the company.

Achievements

After a series of pilot exercises in 1979, London Festival Ballet created its own education and community unit in March 1980. Drawing on the company's wide range of resources, this new department aims to help people to understand and appreciate classical ballet. The unit's activities include a learning materials service, and special programmes to suit individual interests and needs, such as talks, workshops, lecture-demonstrations and

Andria Hall and Ben van Cauwenbergh in Act Two of John Field's production of Swan Lake, *1982.*
Photo: Anthony Crickmay.

short courses which often involve dancers, musicians and other company personnel.

In Spring 1981, the company co-operated with the English National Opera in a special Bartók centenary programme consisting of two ballets and an opera. Later that year, the Arts Council of Great Britain gave financial assistance for a pilot project: the launching of a group of dancers from the company, accompanied by a small orchestra, which would tour a special repertoire to theatres which could not accommodate the whole company. André Prokovsky created *The Storm* for the group, and for the main company he choreographed *Verdi Variations*.

As well as expanding the repertoire, John Field was keen to give younger dancers the opportunity to dance soloist roles in the classics. Two full evening ballets have been added to London Festival Ballet's repertoire. John Field's own production of *Swan Lake*, designed by Carl Toms was premièred at the London Coliseum in May 1982, and John Cranko's *Onegin* at the Palace Theatre, Manchester, in October 1983.

As director of London Festival Ballet, John Field continued to pursue the early policies established by the company's founders: to take classical ballet of a high standard to a wider audience. In September 1984 he was succeeded by Peter Schaufuss.

Suggested Further Reading

There are no publications dealing specifically with the history of London Festival Ballet, although there are personal accounts written about some of the individuals associated with the company, such as:

Braunsweg, J. (1974) *Braunsweg's ballet scandals*, London: George Allen and Unwin.

Dolin, A. (1953) *Markova, her life and art*, London: W. H. Allen.

Dolin, A. (1960) *Autobiography*, London: Oldbourne Books.

Gilpin, J. (1982) *A dance with life*, London: William Kimber.

Gillard, D. (1977) *Beryl Grey*, London: W. H. Allen.

A more detailed booklist is obtainable from the Education and Community Unit at Festival Ballet House. London Festival Ballet has produced souvenir brochures or annuals throughout most of its history, and in particular the 1980 brochure, celebrating the company's thirtieth birthday, contains many photographs illustrating ballets in the company's repertoire. This is obtainable from the publicity department of London Festival Ballet.

London Festival Ballet:
chart showing significant events in the history of the company

1950

Formation of the Festival Ballet (later
renamed London Festival Ballet) by
Anton Dolin, Alicia Markova and
Dr Julian Braunsweg.

1952

L.C.C. invites company to make Royal
Festival Hall a regular performance
venue.

1962

Company awarded grant by L.C.C.

1965

Arts Council intervenes at time of
financial difficulty: Albery takes over as
director.

1968

Beryl Grey takes over as artistic director.

1969

Company begins regular seasons at the
London Coliseum.

1975

Rudolf Nureyev's production of *The
Sleeping Beauty* toured to Australia.

1977

Acquisition of company's first
permanent home: Festival Ballet House.

1979

John Field succeeds Beryl Grey as
director.

1980

Arts Council funds pilot project: small
group of dancers and chamber orchestra
present classical ballet in theatres where
full company cannot be accommodated.

Creation of education and community
unit.

London Festival Ballet: choreochronicle of works mentioned in the chapter

DATE OF FIRST PERFORMANCE BY THE LONDON FESTIVAL BALLET	TITLE	CHOREOGRAPHER	COMPOSER	DESIGNER	DATE OF FIRST PERFORMANCE IF ORIGINALLY PRODUCED ELSEWHERE
1950	The Nutcracker	after Ivanov	Tchaikovsky	Kirsta	Imperial Russian Ballet, St. Petersburg, 1892
1950	Petrouchka	Fokine (Beriozoff)	Stravinsky	after Benois	Diaghilev Ballets Russes, 1911
1950	Giselle	Coralli (Dolin)	Adam	Stevenson	Paris Opéra, 1841
1950	Le Spectre de la Rose	Fokine (Dolin/Karsavina)	Weber (Berlioz)	after Bakst	Diaghilev Ballets Russes, 1911
1951	Prince Igor	Fokine (Beriozoff)	Borodin	Roerich	Diaghilev Ballets Russes, 1909
1952	Schéhérazade	Fokine (Beriozoff)	Rimsky-Korsakoff	after Bakst	Diaghilev Ballets Russes, 1910
1952	Symphony for Fun	Charnley	Gillis	Lingwood	
1955	Etudes	Lander	Czerny (Riisager)	Gerard	Royal Danish Ballet, 1948
1957	The Witch Boy	Carter	Salzedo	McDowell	Ballet der Lage Landen, Amsterdam, 1956
1957	The Nutcracker	Lichine	Tchaikovsky	Benois	Original Ivanov production Imperial Russian Ballet, St. Petersburg, 1892
1959	London Morning	Carter	Coward	McDowell/Constable	
1960	Bourrée Fantasque	Balanchine	Chabrier	Karinska	New York City Ballet, 1949
1961	Swan Lake Act II	Bourmeister after Ivanov	Tchaikovsky	Delany	Original Ivanov production Act II, Imperial Russian Ballet, St. Petersburg, 1894; Bourmeister production, Stanislavsky Theatre Ballet, 1953
1961	The Snow Maiden	Bourmeister	Tchaikovsky	Epishin/Pimenov	
1963	Peer Gynt	Orlikowsky	Grieg	Delany/Lloyd	
1964	Swan Lake	Orlikowsky	Tchaikovsky	Colonello	Choreography after original Petipa/Ivanov, Imperial Russian Ballet, St. Petersburg, 1895

Year	Title	Choreographer	Composer	Designer	Notes
1965	Swan Lake	Orlikowsky	Tchaikovsky	Truscott	As above
1966	Swan Lake	Carter	Tchaikovsky	Truscott	Carter's production first produced at Teatro Colon, Buenos Aires, 1963
1966	The Nutcracker	Carter	Tchaikovsky	after Benois	Original Ivanov production, Imperial Russian Ballet, St. Petersburg, 1892
1966	Noir et Blanc	Lifar	Lalo	McDowell	(As *Suite en Blanc*) Paris Opéra, 1943
1967	Night Shadow	Balanchine	Rieti/Bellini	Farmer	Ballets Russes de Monte Carlo, 1946
1967	The Sleeping Beauty	Stevenson/Grey after Petipa	Tchaikovsky	McDowell	Imperial Russian Ballet, St. Petersburg, 1890
1968	Coppélia	Carter after Saint-Léon	Delibes	Farmer	Paris Opéra, 1870. London Festival Ballet's two-Act production was expanded to three Acts in 1969
1971	Giselle	Skeaping after Perrot, Coralli, Petipa	Adam	Walker	Original production, Paris Opéra, 1841
1971	Le Beau Danube	Massine	Strauss	Polunin/Guy de Beaumont	Soirées de Paris de Comte Etienne de Beaumont, 1924; first production, London Festival Ballet, 1950
1972	Summer Solstice	Moreland	Field	Dunlop	
1973	The Three-Cornered Hat	Massine	de Falla	Picasso	Ballets Russes de Diaghilev, 1919
1973	Gaîté Parisienne	Massine	Offenbach	de Beaumont	Ballet Russes de Monte Carlo, 1938
1973	Echoing of Trumpets	Tudor	Martinu	Beryling	Royal Swedish Ballet, 1963
1974	Parade	Massine	Satie	Picasso	Diaghilev Ballets Russes, 1917
1974	Prodigal Son (in Ragtime)	Moreland	Joplin/Hossak	Annals	
1975	The Sleeping Beauty	Nureyev after Petipa	Tchaikovsky	Georgiadis	Petipa choreography first performed, Imperial Russian Ballet, St. Petersburg, 1890; Nureyev version first staged for La Scala, Milan, 1966
1976	Dancing Space	Moreland	Mozart	Doidge	
1976	The Golden Cockerel	Fokine (Beriozoff)	Rimsky-Korsakoff	Gontcharova	de Basil Original Ballets Russes, 1937

DATE OF FIRST PERFORMANCE BY THE LONDON FESTIVAL BALLET	TITLE	CHOREOGRAPHER	COMPOSER	DESIGNER	DATE OF FIRST PERFORMANCE IF ORIGINALLY PRODUCED ELSEWHERE
1976	Les Sylphides	Fokine (Markova)	Chopin (Douglas)	Guy	First performance under the title Les Sylphides, Diaghilev Ballets Russes, 1909; first production by London Festival Ballet, 1950
1976	The Nutcracker	Hynd	Tchaikovsky	Docherty	Original Ivanov production, Imperial Russian Ballet, St. Petersburg, 1892
1977	Romeo and Juliet	Nureyev	Prokofiev	Frigerio	Stuttgart Ballet, 1975
1978	Greening	Tetley	Nordheim	Baylis	
1979	Rosalinda	Hynd	Strauss (Lanchbery)	Docherty	P.A.C.T., South Africa, 1978
1979	La Sylphide	Schaufuss after Bournonville	Løvenskjold	Walker	Original Bournonville production, Royal Danish Ballet, 1836
1979	Sphinx	Tetley	Martinu	Ter-Arutunian/Kim	American Ballet Theatre, 1977
1980	Journey to Avalon	Moreland	Maxwell-Davies	Baylis	
1981	The Storm	Prokovsky	Shostakovitch	Farmer	
1981	Verdi Variations	Prokovsky	Verdi	Farmer	
1982	Swan Lake	Ivanov/Petipa (Field)	Tchaikovsky	Toms	Original Petipa/Ivanov production, St. Petersburg, 1895
1983	Onegin	Cranko	Tchaikovsky (Stolze)	Rose	Stuttgart Ballet, 1965

Chapter 4

London Contemporary Dance Theatre

Richard Mansfield

For the purpose of this book the history of London Contemporary Dance Theatre is divided into five major periods:

1954–66   the years following the first British performance of the Martha Graham Company, up to the founding by Robin Howard of the London School of Contemporary Dance†, and its parent organisation, Contemporary Ballet Trust‡;

1967–69   the years following the arrival of Robert Cohan as artistic director and the first performance of London Contemporary Dance Group, up until the beginnings of The Place and the first perfomances of London Contemporary Dance Theatre;

1970–75   the years of growth during which the company developed until it no longer needed the support of 'star' dancers from the Martha Graham Company or the works of outside choreographers;

1976–79   a period of expansion and maturity, between the tenth anniversary of the school and the tenth anniversary of the company, and during which The Place doubled in size;

1980–   the years during which some of the senior members of the company left to lead other major companies or form companies of their own, whilst there was an influx of strong young talent from the school.

---

† London School of Contemporary Dance altered its name to London Contemporary Dance School in 1982.

‡ Contemporary Ballet Trust altered its name to Contemporary Dance Trust in 1970.

Introduction

The company in today

London Contemporary Dance Theatre is widely recognised as one of the leading dance companies in Europe. Indeed, as long ago as 1977 one of America's most important dance critics, Walter Terry, said, 'It is, as far as I know, the best modern dance company abroad. I would say it easily ranks on a par with the major modern dance companies in America.'[1]

The company performs regularly in most of the major cities throughout Great Britain, has two annual seasons at Sadler's Wells Theatre in London, and an average of two foreign tours every year. Since its first official perfomances as London Contemporary Dance Theatre in 1969 it has performed in many countries all over the world.

London Contemporary Dance Theatre is comprised of eighteen dancers, although there are occasions when the full complement is twenty-two. The company is lead by a directorate of three: Robert Cohan, responsible for policy and forward planning; Siobhan Davies, resident choreographer; and Janet Eager, administrative director. All three work together with Robin Howard on broad and long-term policy.

The school in today

London Contemporary Dance School is the school to which London Contemporary Dance Theatre is attached and from where it recruits all its dancers. The school is the major centre for the education and training of professional contemporary dancers outside the United States, and it draws its students from every part of the world. 'The establishment of the London School of Contemporary Dance with its widely recognised and respected professional standards is one of the most important developments in British dance education since the war.'[2] The justification of this statement can be shown by the fact that a large majority of the modern dance companies, choreographers, soloists, and teachers in Great Britain have sprung from this school. Leading artistic directors and choreographers include: Robert North, now artistic director of Ballet Rambert; Richard Alston, resident choreographer for Ballet Rambert; Siobhan Davies, co-director of Second Stride; Micha Bergese, artistic director of Mantis; Geoff Powell, founder, and Emilyn Claid, artistic director, of Extemporary Dance Company; Irene Dilks, founder, and Timothy Lamford, artistic director, of

Spiral Dance Company; Ross McKim, co-founder of English Dance Theatre and the Northern School of Contemporary Dance; Shelley Lee, founder and artistic director of Basic Space Dance Company; and the list continues throughout the network of dance companies in this country and abroad.

It is a remarkable fact that in 1984 the school is only eighteen years old, its official opening being May 1966; and the company is just fifteen years old, its first performance as London Contemporary Dance Theatre being in September 1969. Both the school and the company are housed at The Place, under the umbrella title of Contemporary Dance Trust, a charitable organisation set up in 1966 by a man with extraordinary vision and commitment, Robin Howard. The Place now consists of ten dance studios, a 250-seat theatre, music rooms, an audio-visual workshop, a body-conditioning studio, an extensive dance library, and all the many other rooms and offices that are necessary for such a large organisation.

What is more remarkable is that Contemporary Dance Trust and all its blossoming activities ever began at all, and that despite its overwhelming influence on the development of dance throughout Great Britain and elsewhere, it has faced financial bankruptcy several times and will continue to do so until it receives sufficient funding.

Robert Cohan, artistic director of Contemporary Dance Trust, has always believed that the company is only as good as the school which feeds it, and that there is little point in having one without the other. It is, therefore, a fascinating story for the dance historian to consider: an institution which on the one hand has fought for and won worldwide acclaim, and on the other has had to struggle continuously against the most appalling odds.

1954–66: Martha Graham, Robin Howard, and the founding of the school

Martha Graham

In March 1954, the Martha Graham Dance Company performed in Great Britain for the first time. During the early fifties in America, it was unusual for modern dance companies to perform more than one night in each town or city because the dance was thought to be so avant-garde and consequently did not attract large audiences. It was unusual for Graham to have even a New York season of more than one week, despite the fact that what she was presenting was treated very seriously as a new form of art. All the dancers in New York thought that London was the most important place to be accepted and that it was the artistic centre of Europe, so when the Graham Company opened at the Saville Theatre in London it was for what was then a mammoth two-week season. The unfortunate result was that the London critics met the first performance with incomprehension and prejudice, and insisted on calling it 'free dance' or 'barefoot dance'. As Robert Cohan remembers:

We were totally devastated to be completely rejected here – but completely. Almost all the critics, one after another, said that this was an absurd way to move, an absurd idea of dance, there was no technique to start with, it was boring, it was ugly, it was stupid – one review after another. There was one night when there were only thirty people in the audience.[3].

However, among those thirty people were a handful for whom the performances were a revelation, and it was these few eventually who were able to change the course of British dance. One of the first to champion Graham's work was the dance critic for *The Observer*, Richard Buckle, who on the Sunday before the second week wrote: 'Now I conjure every idle, habit-formed fellow, in need of a third eye to see new beauty, that he should visit the Saville Theatre and watch Martha Graham. She is one of the great creators of our time . . . I hope all thoughtful people will see her, for she has enlarged the language of the soul.'[4]

Robin Howard

Among those in the dance world who did take notice of this strange new art form was an extraordinary man, a man who had been so severely injured in the war that he now walked with

114

artificial legs, a man not from the dance profession, but an ardent ballet fan, Robin Howard. And it was to be almost totally due to his enthusiasm and generosity that Graham was to be persuaded to return to London nine years later in 1963. In 1954 he was perhaps one of the 'habit-formed fellows' to whom Buckle had addressed his review. Howard was growing rather tired of seeing the same ballets performed time and time again. As he remembers:

I got a little bored, because by the time you've seen *Swan Lake* a hundred times you want to see something different. I was told by some friends that an American company, the Martha Graham Company, was coming to this country. I'd never heard of it. They told me I probably wouldn't like it, but I went along, and was completely bowled over by it. And I happened to meet a number of the members of the Company, one of whom was Bob Cohan to whom I formed an immediate liking, immediate great, great respect. And that I thought was going to be the end of it.[5]

But that was not to be the end of it – in a very real sense it was just the beginning. In 1963, when Robin Howard was told that Martha Graham's tour of European cities was going to end in Germany and not come to Britain at all, he thought that this was so disgraceful, and felt so personally disappointed, that he made enquiries and eventually arranged to bring the Graham Company to the Edinburgh Festival and then to London. As he remembers:

Edinburgh wasn't arranged until after London, as it happens. I rang up Lord Harewood, who was Director of the Edinburgh Festival at that time, and said 'Will you take the Graham Company?', and he said 'Yes'. I then said 'It looks as if I'm going to lose a lot of money when they're in London, even if you do give them a guarantee in Edinburgh; if it gets more than I can afford will you take some of the loss with me?'. And he said 'Yes' again – which was quite extraordinary.[6]

Mainly through luck it was exactly the right moment, and there were a number of people all in key positions who wanted to help. The ensuing season in Edinburgh was extremely successful, and the glowing reviews from the critics were such that by the time the company arrived for the London season it was very nearly sold out. Graham was an incredible sixty-nine years old and still performing, but a new, young audience was building up for this kind of dance.

Robin Howard, who at that time was doing full-time voluntary work for the United Nations Association, was no professional financier of dance companies; 'Again I thought that was the end of it. But a number of prominent people in the dance world, notably that wonderful lady, Dame Marie Rambert, said to me, "We don't know who you are or why you are doing this, but don't stop now."'[7]

First students

What Dame Marie Rambert and others were asking was that British dancers be enabled to obtain this kind of training. Howard asked Graham and, being very pleased with the trip, she agreed to give free tuition. Howard arranged for an audition to be held, and at first, from the fifteen dancers who applied, Graham chose three; Eileen Cropley, Christian Holder and Anna Price. Eventually others were chosen, but meantime Howard set up a small trust to meet the expenses of travel and maintenance. It must be stated that it can only be said to have been 'small' in comparison to what this man was to pay out later. The first student, Eileen Cropley, arrived in New York on Christmas Day 1963.

Initial policies

Graham's triumphant visit in 1963 was followed rapidly in 1964 by a three-and-a-half-week season of the Merce Cunningham Dance Company, a six-week visit from the Alvin Ailey Dance Company, and, subsidised by Robin Howard, a two-and-a-half-week season by the Paul Taylor Dance Company. It was during the Paul Taylor season that Robin Howard invited all the dance critics to his floating restaurant, The Yard Arm, where he produced a statement of his plans for British dance and asked for alternative suggestions. His intention was to encourage the existing dance scene, not to create a new organisation; it was 'to enable people in this country to keep in touch with developments elsewhere and to experiment more themselves'.[8] This was to be done by sending more students to the United States, as Graham had agreed by this time to give free tuition for up to ten students a year. Additionally, it was intended that more companies should be brought to Britain, and teachers from America should be invited here also. British companies would receive financial support, a scheme that Howard had already begun with companies such as Ballet Rambert, Ballet-makers, and Norman McDowell's London Dance Theatre. However, it is the final paragraph of Howard's 1964 proposal which now sounds so prophetic: 'If there is sufficient support, a permanent studio will be set up, open to established teachers of modern dance. Later still, a small touring company may be helped to start, but only if there is a need for it and there is room for it. It is also intended eventually to arrange exchanges with countries other than the United States.'[9]

Guest teachers from America
In the following April, 1965, Mary Hinkson was the first of three leading dancers from the Graham Company to arrive in Britain to begin teaching classes for the next three months. The other two following closely behind were Ethel Winter and Bertram Ross. Eileen Cropley, the first of the British students to train with Graham, was used as a demonstrator. In July, they took part in a joint venture with The Royal Ballet, a week of lecture-demonstration performances of Ballet for All at the Theatre Royal, Stratford East. It was a great success, the houses were packed, and for Robin Howard this was a real turning-point. The Graham dancers were very experienced performers, in contrast to The Royal Ballet dancers who had only just graduated from the Royal Ballet School; thus although they subsequently became very fine dancers, at this time they looked less accomplished than Hinkson, Winter and Ross who were sharing half the programme with them. Peter Brinson, founder of Ballet for All, acted as the commentator while the dancers demonstrated the technique and showed extracts from Graham's repertoire. His script opened as follows: 'Behind classical ballet lie three hundred years and more of development. Behind Graham lie thirty years – or at the most sixty, if you include the forerunners of today's modern dance, like Isadora Duncan.'[10] It went on to state that the Graham 'approach' had begun as a revolt against the restrictions that had seemed inseparable from classical ballet at the beginning of the century. The Graham approach, as with all the other modern dance movements, had grown out of a need to explore the expressive possibilities of the human body beyond that which had been achieved by classical ballet. 'Today, revolt has been replaced by collaboration. Graham's contemporary dance incorporates much from the classical ballet. The ballet recognises the value of much of what Graham has added to the dance. This is why we think it worthwhile to show you some of the discoveries of each, side by side on the same stage.'[11] At the close of the programme Brinson's last line spoke of 'two points of view, two funds of experience, but one single art – the dance'. It was this attitude of mutual respect, expressed publicly at a time when there was still much hostility from the ballet world, that was one of the most important developments thus far in Robin Howard's plans.

Regular London-based classes

With the success of the Ballet for All series, it became obvious that there was a need for permanent good teachers in London. In September 1965, permanent classes began with Eileen Cropley as principal teacher. It was now twenty-one months since she had arrived in New York to begin her training with Graham. The nucleus of those who began classes when 'the school', as it was beginning to be called, came together on a continuing basis in September, were chosen by a committee of prominent people in the dance world. Twelve students constituted that nucleus. There was no permanent home for them but they represented the beginning of regular London-based classes, and the first sign of independence with the school being able to operate for short periods of time without American teachers. The school would not be truly independent for another ten years, but it was the beginning.

Reporting on what it had learned in the last two years, and particularly during the last nine months, a small committee led by Marie Rambert met in January. In this committee's report it was stated that the Martha Graham approach and technique was suitable for British dancers, and it was recommended that regular classes of the highest artistic standards be started in London as soon as possible.

Berners Place

In response to this and with the school having moved from studio to studio throughout London, Robin Howard found temporary quarters for it in Berners Place, at the back of Oxford Street.There was one studio, one room with a small library, and very primitive washing facilities. Thus, in May 1966, the London School of Contemporary Dance opened officially. That May, 1966, *Dance And Dancers* declared, 'Robin Howard's new venture will be called The London School of Contemporary Dance . . . It may take time for the results of all this to become apparent, but it has all the signs of those unassuming academies formed by Dames Ninette de Valois and Marie Rambert way back in the twenties – and we all know where they led to.'[12]

The Trust

On 18 July 1966, Contemporary Ballet Trust was formed. It was decided to use the word 'ballet' because 'dance' at that time was seen to be only connected with dance halls, and Robin Howard was advised that it would be impossible to obtain trust status if this word were used. In most circles, 'ballet' was considered legitimately 'serious', whereas 'dance' was thought frivolous and slightly immoral. Eventually, in 1970, it would be safe to alter the name to Contemporary Dance Trust. The Trust was formed to control the school, which Howard founded under the patronage of Martha Graham, John Gielgud, Dames Ninette de Valois and Marie Rambert, Lord Harewood and Henry Moore. Its guiding purpose was to supply the needs which seemed to be growing in Britain for this radically different kind of training for dancers.

The policy

The policy was 'to be of service to and through the dance'. In the October of that year, 1966, Robin Howard commented, 'Our object is not to try and transplant American modern dance to this country; it is to try and develop a native style appropriate to the bodies and outlook of British people, to our climate and the rest of our culture. We have chosen to base it upon the Graham approach and technique because we feel that this is far more developed than any alternative – it is out and away the best.'[13]

Howard then went on to describe how the idea of a company was beginning to emerge; he stated that the original aim had been to train the dancers whom someone else would form into a company. 'At the moment there is no obvious genius to do this. What we may do is to create a company . . . I hope to back it, and encourage the choreographers. We hope a great choreographer will come along, but, if not, we must use the best that are about.'[14] With the benefit of hindsight these seem prophetic words indeed, especially in the year when Robert Cohan had just become a co-director of the Graham Company.

The importance of the developments in London was beginning to be felt even at this early stage. Clive Barnes, while reviewing *Mary Wigman at Eighty*, in the *New York Times* wrote, 'In Europe she [Wigman] is still teaching, but no one takes much notice. The new but still powerful hope of European modern dance is based exclusively on the Martha Graham school in London.'[15] In the meantime Ballet Rambert had completely reorganised and, on 28 November 1966, gave its first performance of contemporary works at the Jeanetta Cochrane Theatre.

1967–69: Robert Cohan, first performances by the students, the beginnings of The Place, and the first performance of London Contemporary Dance Theatre

The school was expanding and managing to produce good enough student dancers to give supporting performances with Yuriko Amamaya, an ex-Graham dancer, and to perform the choreographic work of their teachers with Balletmakers, a group of choreographers, composers and designers who presented experimental workshop performances. Also the students themselves held their own workshop performances. But the organisation lacked artistic direction, and this really became clear to Howard after many of the students had taken part in the danced Mass at the official opening of Liverpool Cathedral. The performance had not reached the standard for which he had hoped.

I learned from Liverpool that we needed a strong figure. Graham came back here in the Spring of '67, and I said I wanted the impossible, a great teacher, an unselfish person who would help bring others forward rather than himself, and that awful word leadership – someone who would make a significant contribution as a dancer and a choreographer without dominating too much. Bob was the only one in the entire dance scene who fitted these categories.[16]

Robert Cohan

After hearing Howard's plans Robert Cohan agreed to become artistic director of the Trust, spending half his time in London and the other half with the Graham Company. This was June, and the immediate challenge he faced was to present a week of performances at the Adeline Genée Theatre in East Grinstead. The first money ever given to the Trust by other than private sources was £2,000 from the Arts Council specially for this project. Originally the season was to be held during July, but when Cohan saw the people he would be using, students in the top class at the School, he postponed it until the October. As Cohan remembers:

'I said to Robin . . . I choreograph the dances now, and we do nothing except rehearse them for four months. They won't be able to dance, but they'll be able to do those dances very well. Maybe we'll get away with it.'[17]

Cohan choreographed *Sky* and *Tzaikerk* in the summer of 1967 for the students, but with the leading roles being danced by Robert Powell and Noemi Lapsezon, who were both dancers with the Graham Company and had performed in Cohan's own company in the early sixties. Cohan danced also. Two other works by Cohan, *Eclipse* and *Hunter of Angels*, were put into the programme. There were also works by some of the student dancers, David Earle, Anna Mittelholzer and Patrick Steede. The company was named London Contemporary Dance Group, and two of the youngest members were Robert North and Namron. Linda Gibbs joined soon after the season finished, Siobhan Davies had a walk-on part and she and Richard Alston helped backstage.

On 10 October 1967, in East Grinstead, the Group gave its first performance, and was greeted with tremendous enthusiasm from both press and public alike. *The Times Educational Supplement* for November declared, 'The achievement was remarkable. In *Sky* and *Tzaikerk* the ensemble performance was of a quality which showed at once that British temperaments can master the language, and Britain can have a modern dance company'.[18]

For the next one and a half years the Group toured the British Isles, performing in schools, colleges, universities and community halls. The purpose was not only to entertain, explain the principles of Graham-based technique, and recruit students and sponsors, but also to give the dancers performing experience. As Robert North remembers:

'We got £7 a week. But it was a marvellous time in the beginning; the studio and the Company were all one unit, and some very good students came out of the first year. We had Sue [Siobhan Davies], Richard [Alston], Celeste [Dandeker], Paula [Lansley] – all out of the first year.'[19]

Policy

In the September of 1968, the Trust re-organised the school and offered a full-time three-year course, the aim of which was to create an educated 'artist dancer'. Since 1968 the idea of the thinking 'artist dancer' has been central to all the school's work. As Cohan had said in the September edition of *Dance and Dancers* the previous year in 1967: 'It is not sufficient to be a good dancer, you have to think, and you have to know what dance is all about . . . Without that you cannot put enough meaning into your work. It's not enough to stretch your legs, you have to stretch your mind.

Otherwise it all comes out as just movement with no image, no life in it.'[20]

The Arts Council grant was increased to £5,000 with a hint that there would be substantial financial assistance from that organisation if the Trust, whose lease at Berners Place was coming up for renewal, were to find a larger permanent home. The one studio at Berners was constantly in use and could not deal with the growing demand for space. Howard set about finding a suitable building.

1969: The Trust moves into The Place, and London Contemporary Dance Theatre makes its début

---

In January 1969, Howard wrote to Cohan, who was in New York, and said that he had found an extraordinary building, but that it was much too large. Cohan flew back to England, and Howard took Jane Dudley and William Louther to view the recently vacated Headquarters and Drill Hall of the 21st S.A.S. Regiment (Artists) Territorial Army, near Euston Station. All agreed it was ideal. However, the thought of going from one studio to six was an extremely difficult decision, and that decision was not made easier when it came to the moment of signing the lease. The lease was for nine and a half years on the assumption that by the time it ran out the school and company would be established, and be able to get another building, or it would be bankrupt. The Trust nearly went bankrupt several times during that period, not least during the first year at The Place, as it was to be called. There was an opening ceremony for the official signing of the lease, and just as Howard was about to sign a representative from the Arts Council handed him a piece of paper;

> It was a note from the Arts Council saying that they were very sorry but there wasn't the money they'd told me there might be. That was literally at the moment of signing. Well, I've never been a good administrator but I've never been afraid, I think, of taking a chance. So we went ahead as if I hadn't read it, and we had our opening ceremony. But we did in fact run out of money.'[21]

Alterations began during the Easter, and Anthony van Laast remembers as a student helping to paint walls and remove rubble for five shillings an hour.

In the summer, the Trust moved into the building, and on 2nd September, with the Group having toured Scotland, England and France, the London Contemporary Dance Company began its first

Cell, 1969. *Choreography by Robert Cohan. Dancers from left to right: Robert North, Xenia Hribar, Linda Gibbs, Anthony van Laast, Siobhan Davies and Ross McKim.* The Sunday Telegraph *writer commented that it was nothing short of a masterpiece.*
Photo: Anthony Crickmay.

London season in The Place Theatre. These were the first performances of London Contemporary Dance Theatre. The Company was strengthened by stars from the Graham Company, Noemi Lapzeson, Robert Powell, William Louther and Cohan himself. The programme included Martha Graham's *El Penitente*, Cohan's *Side Scene, Shanta Quintet* and *Cell*, Barry Moreland's *Cortège* and *Hosannas* and Alvin Ailey's *Hermit Songs* among others. The season, which ran for three weeks, met with enthusiasm from the press. *The Sunday Telegraph*, of Cohan's *Cell*, said that it was nothing short of a masterpiece and continued, 'This group should become one of our major dance assets now its School is established and its demonstration tours have whetted our appetite . . . If we are to see American modern dance, then we need to see major achievements with first rate dancers, and the Contemporary Dance Theatre is in a position to give us both.'[22]

Directly after the season, Robin Howard called a press conference and announced that the Trust had run out of money, and unless the Arts Council changed its mind the Trust would close down on 31st December. Nothing happened for three months, until 21st December, when Howard received a telephone call from the Gulbenkian Foundation saying that his application for money had been accepted, and that Contemporary Ballet Trust would receive a grant of £30,000 to be spread over three years. Then on Christmas Eve 1969, he received a call from the Arts Council,

'saying that the money they had said was not there in January had been discovered and was available after all. I was able to tell the Company that we were not closing down, but that there would be no money from either source until April 1st, 1970.'[23]

At the time of the first season Robert Cohan decided to stop commuting across the Atlantic; he thought the situation unfair for both the Graham Company and the Trust. He chose England because he realised that whenever he left New York the Graham Company continued without problems whereas whenever he left London everything stopped until he returned.

1970–75: the development of the company and the gaining of independence

Despite the fact that the whole organisation was forced to continue with no money until the grants from the Arts Council and the Gulbenkian Foundation were due to arrive in April 1970, it was possible by March of that year to offer the dancers a full year's employment. Nevertheless, at this stage it was still only a semi-permanent company. During this year the entire company took part in other London seasons; four weeks during May and June; two weeks during October. For the rest of the year the company was divided into two sections; six members were based in London to continue the teaching, workshops and experimental work, and the other twelve constituted a touring section for performances in Britain and abroad.

This year, 1970, saw the first of Robert North's works to be taken into the company repertoire, *Conversation Piece*. Ballet for All included a new programme incorporating dancers from the company. Juliet Fisher, an ex-Graham dancer, began these tours, and taught the work to Siobhan Davies, who took over after about nine months.

Despite the fact that Robert Cohan, and Pat Hutchinson, who was then principal of the school, thought that the Trust had done well to become so established in such a short time, they thought that the contemporary teaching in the school was not of a sufficiently high standard. It was thus that Jane Dudley was invited to become Director of Graham Studies. This title was later changed during the mid-seventies to Director of Contemporary Dance Studies.

1971, Stages

In April 1971 the company presented Cohan's first full-length work, *Stages*, as part of the Camden Festival. The work was based on the myth of the hero and its relation to contemporary society. The result was a multimedia event with stunning lighting effects, changes of costume, gymnastics, and a whole host of other ingredients that appealed directly to young people. It had the same kind of effect that a rock concert has on its audience. It became an extraordinary success, and it was largely due to this work that over the next two years many young people became interested in contemporary dance.

Stages, 1971. *Choreography by Robert Cohan. Dancers: Robert North (centre standing) and members of the company. The extraordinary success of* Stages *was largely responsible for many young people becoming interested in contemporary dance.*
Photo: Colin Clarke.

In 1972, the Trust received financial assistance not only from the Arts Council and the Gulbenkian Foundation, but also from the Greater London Council, and the London Borough of Camden. In response the company presented no less than eighteen new works, including *Tiger Balm* by Richard Alston, *One Was The Other* by Robert North and Noemi Lapzeson, *Brian* by Robert North, *Kontakion* by Barry Moreland, *Relay* by Siobhan Davies, *Outside-In* by Micha Bergese and Anthony van Laast, and *People Alone* by Robert Cohan. The policy of encouraging work from within the company was supplemented by the use of outside choreographers such as Remy Charlip, May O'Connell and Anna Sokolow.

Strider, the first new group

By September 1972, there were 120 full-time students in the school, and 200 part-time students, whilst Nina Fonaroff, from New York, had arrived to re-organise the teaching of choreography. It was in this year also that Richard Alston, who had been one of the first students at the school and had led the Trust's 'X Group', choreographing for the lecture-demonstrations that it gave, decided to form his own company, Strider. This, for Robin Howard, was one of the most important moments in the history of the Trust, the setting up from within the school of a breakaway company. It represented the first independent company founded by a former student. Alston himself described the new company as a 'home for tall rejects'. Their rehearsals were held at The Place, they made their début there, and Robin Howard drew up their initial budget and nominated them for a grant from the Gulbenkian Foundation. During the same year, 1972, Siobhan Davies had her first work taken into the company repertory, *Relay*.

In the July of 1973 the school was approved officially by the Department of Education and Science as an establishment of Further Education, and this meant that many prospective students were more likely to acquire grants from local education authorities in order to pay for their training. At the same time, negotiations began for new premises, although they were eventually dropped in favour of extending the existing premises at The Place.

Meanwhile, the company was going from strength to strength. It continued its extensive British touring, but added a seven-and-a-half-week tour of South America. This was followed by a summer season at The Place, with new works by Alston and Cohan, and then a twelve-week tour of *Stages* including the first performance at London's Sadler's Wells Theatre.

During 1974 Robert North and Siobhan Davies were made associate choreographers with the company, and presented two

The Calm, 1974. Choreography by Siobhan Davies. Dancers: Siobhan Davies and Namron.
Photo: Anthony Crickmay.

Troy Game, 1974. *Choreography by Robert North. Dancers from left to right: Jean-Louis Morin, Robert North, Namron, Ross McKim, Anthony van Laast and Micha Bergese.* Troy Games, *an all-male display of rhythm, strength and stamina, proved to be so popular with audiences everywhere that it was eventually taken to the repertories of The Royal Ballet and the Dance Theatre of Harlem.*
Photo: Anthony Crickmay.

new works each; Siobhan Davies, *Pilot* and *The Calm*; Robert North, *Dressed To Kill* and *Troy Game*. *Troy Game*, an all-male display of rhythm, strength and stamina, proved to be so popular with audiences everywhere that it was eventually taken into the repertories of The Royal Ballet and the Dance Theatre of Harlem. In addition there were three new works by Robert Cohan, one by Richard Alston, and several works by outside choreographers including Anna Sokolow, Dan Waggoner and Martha Graham.

During the summer tour of France, Switzerland, Germany and Belgium, Cohan, at the time suffering from a back injury, decided not to perform again. The fact that the company was able to perform Graham's *Diversion of Angels* (1948), a work of extreme technical difficulty, without any of the ex-Graham Company 'stars' demonstrated how very soon London Contemporary Dance Theatre had matured under Cohan's teaching. By this time the main core of those dancers who were to remain in the company for several years had been formed; Robert North, Namron, Linda Gibbs, Siobhan Davies, Paula Lansley, Anca Frankenhaeuser, Micha Bergese, Kate Harrison, Ross McKim, Anthony van Laast, Cathy Lewis, Celia Hulton, Patrick Harding-Irmer, Charlotte Milner, and joining the very next year, 1975, were Christopher Bannerman, Sallie Estep, Charlotte Kirkpatrick and Tom Jobe.

The company's 1974, three-week season at Sadler's Wells Theatre received very encouraging reviews. *The Evening Standard* in November wrote that since its beginnings in 1967 the company had evolved into 'one of the world's most exhilarating modern dance groups'. In the same month, *The Guardian* wrote that until recently only a small and specialised audience had existed for modern dance but now all that had changed; what was so important about the current Sadler's Wells season was that the modern dance idiom had created a large enough audience to fill the same house that had recently presented the Sadler's Wells Royal Ballet and which was favoured by visiting foreign dance companies.

In 1975 Robin Howard received the Queen Elizabeth Coronation Award for his services to the Art of Ballet, while Robert Cohan, on behalf of the company, received the Evening Standard Award for the Most Outstanding Achievement in Ballet. This year the company produced another eleven works from within its own ranks, and during a mammoth five-week Sadler's Wells season presented a wealth of original choreography. Guest artists included Lynn Seymour, Wayne Sleep and William Louther. Robert Cohan presented *Class, Masque of Separation, Place of Change* and *Stabat Mater*, four works of such artistic strength that they have never left the repertory.

By this time Cohan and the company had found that the technique, which had originally been very much based in the Graham technique, had changed and that a new way of working had evolved. Working together every day Cohan and the dancers had found what naturally suited them and their work. Certainly the results of their technique and their choreographic work were superb, the Sadler's Wells season representing a major event for modern dance in England; the longest season in the largest house so far, and very nearly full every night.

1976–79: A period of expansion and maturity, between the tenth anniversary of the school and the tenth anniversary of the company, and during which The Place doubles in size

Residencies
In the 1976 New Year's Honours List Robin Howard was awarded the C.B.E. That January the company began the first 'residencies' ever to be seen in the United Kingdom. The idea, introduced by Cohan and encouraged by Howard, was for the company to spend a week at a time in five colleges or universities, performing, giving lecture-demonstrations, open classes, open choregraphic sessions, and discussions, with dancers travelling out to teach in local schools, and school parties coming in to meet the company. The purpose was to break down the barriers that seemed to exist between the dance theatre world and that of education. During that first five-week residency in Yorkshire, Cohan choreographed *Khamsin* in public. Since this first venture, residencies in many shapes and forms have become very important for many of the arts.

During that year, 1976, the company worked extremely hard, producing nine new dance works and performing for over thirty-two weeks. The dancers were all appearing every night and most had been taking solo parts. Twenty-six of those weeks had been touring weeks, and the strain was beginning to be too much. Nevertheless at the annual Sadler's Wells season fourteen works were performed, all choreographed by members of the company and none earlier than 1974. New works included Cohan's *Nympheas*, Bergese's *Nema*, and Davies' *Step At A Time*.

Policy to expand The Place
It was in this year that the Trust bought the freehold to The Place and the adjoining buildings in Flaxman Terrace. Building work began to convert the newly acquired premises into additional studios, changing rooms and office facilities. The result would be that The Place, which was too small to contain the school, the company, the evening school, and the children and teenagers classes, would more than double in size. The financial burden of taking on this vast operation was terrifying, but the opportunity and the timing were absolutely perfect.

In the summer, the Trust arranged for the Martha Graham Company to perform at the Royal Opera House, Covent Garden. This was the first time any modern dance company had ever performed there, and was a very firm statement of respect for the artistic standards achieved by Graham and all that she represented.

It was during this period that the Trust decided to drop the term 'Graham technique' when referring to classes taught by members of the school and company. Although based on many of Graham's principles, the contemporary dance technique, a term which covered several versions developed within the school and company, had by this point taken on its own life. As Cohan had said at the time,

I was fascinated, and still am, with the problem of whether you can take a technique, or a concept which becomes a technique, a concept of dance which is really indigenous to the United States, take that and teach it in such a way that it can become translated, and also in time transform and become indigenous to Great Britain. That's always been the object of the exercise.[24]

1977 The United States Tour

In July 1977, almost ten years to the day since Cohan had first started training the Group for its initial performances at East Grinstead, the company departed for the United States to present *Cell, Class, Stabat Mater* and *Masque of Separation* by Cohan, *Diary* by Siobhan Davies, and *Troy Game* by Robert North. The company had been invited to perform at the American Dance Festival in Connecticut. It was a daunting prospect, but an assured success from the first night when the company received a standing ovation from an audience largely comprised of people from the American dance scene. *The Philadelphia Inquirer* wrote that the company was 'already of world class', and *The New York Times* stated, 'Whatever the London Contemporary Dance Theatre is, it is different – different from other modern dance companies and always exciting . . . The major development is the emergence of Robert Cohan as a highly individual choreographer of unusual scope and depth.'[25]

Thus, during the year of its tenth anniversay the company had proven itself to be the equal of any in the world. During the company's Sadler's Wells season *The Sunday Times* wrote, 'In a decade they have implanted modern dance into once alien soil, created and educated a large audience, and established a school whose alumni have already permeated practically every contemporary dance troupe you can think of . . .'[26] The appointment of Micha Bergese as an associate choreographer reaffirmed the policy of encouraging the creation of choreographic works from within the ranks of the company.

In 1978 the company produced fifteen new works from nine of its members. Works included *Eos* and *Ice* by Robert Cohan, *Just Before* by Anthony van Laast, *9 – 5* by Tom Jobe, *Three Solos* by Linda Gibbs, *Solo Ride* by Micha Bergese, *Then You Can Only Sing* by Siobhan Davies, *Scriabin Preludes* and *Dreams With Silences* by Robert North, and the first works for the company by Christopher Bannerman, *Treading* and *Sandsteps*. The company had toured fifteen theatres throughout the country, had performed in London, and had travelled to Egypt. However, the year had proven to be one of increasing difficulty. The main problem had been the strain of so much work and particularly so much touring. The strain was felt by those company members who had been touring for some years, who were perhaps also choreographers, and those who had family responsibilities. Another difficulty was the fact that the rate of inflation was greater than the rise in the annual grant income.

Solo Ride, 1978. *Choreography by Micha Bergese. Dancers from left to right: Tom Jobe, Charlotte Kirkpatrick, Anita Griffin. The appointment of Micha Bergese as associate choreographer reaffirmed the policy of encouraging the creation of choreographic works from within the ranks of the company. Photo: Anthony Crickmay.*

The cost of materials, travel, and of everything upon which the company relied for its creative efforts, had increased alarmingly while at the same time the company was unable to increase its salaries. Meanwhile the cost of converting the Flaxman Building was spiralling. Work was suspended while more money was sought.

However, during a year when the company had introduced 'split touring' whereby the company divided in half for some of the time and performed in twice as many places, Robert Cohan was presented by the Society of West End Theatres with the Award for the Outstanding Achievement of the Year in Ballet.

Tenth anniversary 1979

The company, preferring to think of this year as its tenth anniversary, ten years since the company first performed as London Contemporary Dance Theatre at The Place, had by this time created over 100 dance works, and a new and enthusiastic following had been developed throughout the country. During 1979 over 145,000 people had attended performances and approximately six million had seen the company on television. In his opening remarks for the Sadler's Wells programme of that year, Robin Howard claimed, 'Now we start our second decade. The Company as individuals and as a unit are seeking new ways of working to allow more time and freedom to develop the "creative" spirit which is an integral part of our Company philosophy. Robert Cohan, Siobhan Davies and Robert North have accepted commissions to choreograph works for other companies, Linda Gibbs and Kate Harrison plan to spend four months in America, Namron and Anthony van Laast both intend to devote more time to teaching . . . Just as our Company members are now ready to widen their experiences, so the Company as such is once more ready to work with one or two choreographers from outside.'[27]

This start of the company's 'second decade' saw Micha Bergese leave to pursue free-lance work, although he remained an associate choreographer.

OVERLEAF: Treading, 1978. *Choreography by Christopher Bannerman. Dancers: Christopher Bannerman and Sallie Estep. Christopher Bannerman has been a major choreographer with the company since 1978. Photo: Anthony Crickmay.*

1980–: an influx of young talent from the school

Micha Bergese's departure and that of others soon after in the following year, 1980, coincided with an influx of talented young dancers from the school. During the same period Moshe Romano, the rehearsal director, decided to leave and his replacement was Lenny Westerdijk, who had been a soloist with Ballet Rambert. It is interesting to note that in the same year Richard Alston joined Ballet Rambert as Resident Choreographer. During 1980, the Trust moved finally into the new studios, which provided room not only for the school, the company, and all the other many activities of the Trust, but also for the Rambert School of Ballet. However, the Trust, and in particular the school, were facing a grave crisis. Despite the fact that the school was growing from strength to strength, increasing its numbers, improving its curriculum, and producing dancers of higher quality than ever before, many students were finding it impossible to obtain grants from their local education authorities. The school's only source of income lay in its fees; without them it would have to close. Robert Cohan was quoted in the press as saying, 'The policy has always been to take the dancers for the company from the school and that policy will not change. If the school goes then the feeding ground for the company goes and I don't see the point of one without the other.'[28]

The Trust launched an appeal on behalf of the school, and by a happy coincidence the *Gulbenkian Report on Dance Education and Training in Great Britain* was published soon after. It was an independent report which among the recommendations suggested that on no account should the London School of Contemporary Dance be allowed to close. It ranked the school on the same level of excellence as that of the Royal Ballet School and pointed out that it had to sustain this level of excellence without the degree of national and local authority support on which the Royal Ballet Upper School could usually depend.

In this year, 1980, the last direct links with Martha Graham were broken, and she ceased to be a patron of the Trust. It was a sad but necessary break, one that had been planned with her from the very earliest stages of the Trust's development.

By the end of 1980 the company had completed a seven-and-a-half-week European tour, and had embarked on 'large-scale' touring throughout Great Britain. This meant that the company had increased its audiences by so much that it was required to perform in the largest theatres in the country. In order to maintain its links with the smaller theatres it continued its policy of 'split touring' during parts of the year. It continued to allow dancers time off to work with other choreographers or to choreograph on their own, and provided members of the company for more residencies and work in the education field.

In 1981, Robert North became the artistic director of Ballet Rambert, and Siobhan Davies, although not leaving the company altogether, created her own dance company, 'Siobhan Davies and Dancers'. Robert Cohan took a seven-month sabbatical in the safe knowledge that the company had matured to such an extent that the older members were well equipped to maintain the highest artistic standards. Indeed, during his absence and the company's Workshop Season of New Choreography at The Place, twelve of the fourteen works produced were by dancers in the company. As a result, five were taken into the main repertory.

When Cohan returned he choreographed his second full-length work, *Dances of Love and Death*, for the first visit by the company to the International Edinburgh Festival, the festival at which eighteen years earlier Martha Graham had performed, and during which she agreed to provide free tuition for British dancers. The wheel had turned full-circle.

During 1982, Cohan spent more time away from the company, teaching and choreographing in many parts of the world, while Patrick Harding-Irmer led the company as Acting Artistic Director. The company presented more works of its own but also those of outside choreographers; *The Brood* by Dick Kutch, the duet from *Changing Your Mind* by Dan Waggoner, and *Esplanade* by Paul Taylor. *Esplanade* was taught to the dancers in the company by Eileen Cropley, the very first student sent by Robin Howard to the Graham School in 1963

In September 1982, the school introduced an Honours Degree in Contemporary Dance validated by the University of Kent, giving young prospective professional contemporary dancers an opportunity to obtain an Honours Degree through the practical and professional training in contemporary dance for which the school is internationally respected.

In May 1983, twenty years after Robin Howard had sent the first student to New York and just sixteen years since the first performances at East Grinstead, London Contemporary Dance Theatre made its triumphant New York début at the Brooklyn Academy of

Music as part of the 'Britain Salutes New York' Festival. It was on this high note that Robert Cohan retired as full-time artistic director. In his new role as one of a directorate of three, he works with the company on a half-yearly basis and continues to have responsibility for planning and artistic policy. Siobhan Davies acts as resident choreographer, and Janet Eager, as administrative director, controls the day-to-day running of London Contemporary Dance Theatre. Meanwhile, Sallie Estep has been appointed assistant to the rehearsal director, and Moshe Romano has returned as assistant to the directors. A new era has begun.

The ideas which Robin Howard expressed in his 1964 proposals for modern dance are now, miraculously, working realities. In 1964, he had said, 'If there is sufficient support a permanent studio will be set up, open to established teachers of modern dance. Later still, a small touring company may be helped to start, but only if there is a need for it and there is room for it.'[29] Today, we can look back and see that indeed there was room and need for such a studio and company, although, despite Robin Howard's modest plans, the 'studio' is now a full-time school ranked in importance with that of The Royal Ballet, and the company is claimed to be one of the most creative and exciting modern dance companies in the world.

References

1. Terry, W. (1977) *Saturday Review* 3 September, p.41.
2. Calouste Gulbenkian Foundation (1980) *Dance education and training in Great Britain* London: Gulbenkian, p. 139.
3. Cohan, R. (1979) Speaking at a forum on 50 years of contemporary dance.
4. Buckle, R. (1954) *The Observer*, 23 August.
5. Howard, R. (1977) Speaking in a recorded interview with John Aimis, transmitted in August on Radio 4.
6. Howard, R. (1979) Speaking in an unpublished interview with Richard Mansfield.
7. Howard, R. (1964) Statement of aims. Policy document held by London Contemporary Dance Trust.
8. *Ibid.*
9. *Ibid.*
10. Brinson, P. (1965) Unpublished Ballet for All script.
11. *Ibid.*

12. Anon. (1966) A new force in dance. *Dance and Dancers* May, p. 9.
13. Howard, R. (1966) Transatlantic influence. *Dance and Dancers* October, pp. 28–31.
14. *Ibid.*
15. Barnes, C. (1966) Mary Wigman at eighty. *New York Times* November.
16. Howard, R. (1979) Speaking in an unpublished interview with Richard Mansfield.
17. Cohan, R. (1979) Speaking at a forum on 50 years of contemporary dance.
18. Anon. (1967) *The Times Educational Supplement* November.
19. North, R. (1977) Speaking in a recorded interview with John Aimis, transmitted in August on Radio 4.
20. Cohan, R. (1967) Robert Cohan talks to Dance and Dancers on Contemporary Dance in Britain. *Dance and Dancers* September, pp. 19–21.
21. Howard, R. (1979) Speaking at a forum on 50 years of contemporary dance.
22. Anon. (1969) Review. *The Sunday Telegraph* September.
23. Howard, R. (1979) Speaking at a forum on 50 years of contemporary dance.
24. Cohan, R. (1977) Speaking in a recorded interview with John Aimis, transmitted in August on Radio 4.
25. Kisselgoff, A. (1977) Review. *The New York Times* July.
26. Dougill, D. (1977) Harvest from Martha's Vineyard. *The Sunday Times* 27 November.
27. Howard, R. (1979) Sadler's Wells Theatre programme. November.
28. Cohan, R. (1979) *The Stage and Television Today* June.
29. Howard, R. (1964) Statement of aims. Policy document held by London Contemporary Dance Trust.

Suggested further reading

Brinson, P. and Crisp, C. (1981) *The Pan book of ballet and dance*, London: Pan Books.
McDonagh, D. (1973) *Martha Graham*, Newton Abbot: David and Charles.
Murray, J. (1979) *Dance now*, London: Penguin Books.
For information, articles on the company in various magazines and periodicals write to the Education Department at The Place.

London Contemporary Dance Theatre:
chart showing significant events in the history of the company.

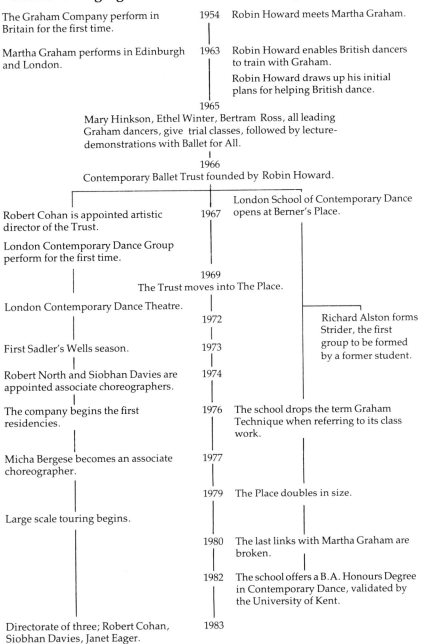

The Graham Company perform in Britain for the first time. | **1954** | Robin Howard meets Martha Graham.

Martha Graham performs in Edinburgh and London. | **1963** | Robin Howard enables British dancers to train with Graham.

Robin Howard draws up his initial plans for helping British dance.

1965

Mary Hinkson, Ethel Winter, Bertram Ross, all leading Graham dancers, give trial classes, followed by lecture-demonstrations with Ballet for All.

1966

Contemporary Ballet Trust founded by Robin Howard.

London School of Contemporary Dance opens at Berner's Place.

Robert Cohan is appointed artistic director of the Trust. | **1967**

London Contemporary Dance Group perform for the first time.

1969

The Trust moves into The Place.

London Contemporary Dance Theatre. | **1972**

Richard Alston forms Strider, the first group to be formed by a former student.

First Sadler's Wells season. | **1973**

Robert North and Siobhan Davies are appointed associate choreographers. | **1974**

The company begins the first residencies. | **1976** | The school drops the term Graham Technique when referring to its class work.

Micha Bergese becomes an associate choreographer. | **1977**

1979 | The Place doubles in size.

Large scale touring begins.

1980 | The last links with Martha Graham are broken.

1982 | The school offers a B.A. Honours Degree in Contemporary Dance, validated by the University of Kent.

Directorate of three; Robert Cohan, Siobhan Davies, Janet Eager. | **1983**

London Contemporary Dance Theatre: choreochronicle of works mentioned in the chapter

DATE OF FIRST PERFORMANCE BY L.C.D.T	TITLE	CHOREOGRAPHER	COMPOSER	DESIGNER	DATE OF FIRST PERFORMANCE IF ORIGINALLY PRODUCED ELSEWHERE
1967	Tzaikerk	Robert Cohan	Alan Hovhaness	Peter Farmer	
1967	Sky	Robert Cohan	Eugene Lester	Walter Martin	
1967	Eclipse	Robert Cohan	Eugene Lester	Michael Robinson	
1967	Hunter of Angels	Robert Cohan	Bruno Maderna	Charles Dunlop	
1967	Witness of Innocence	David Earle	Grazyna Bacowicz		
1967	Family of Man	Anna Mittelholzer	Judyth Knight		
1967	Piece for Metronome and Three Dancers	Patrik Steede			
1969	El Penitente	Martha Graham	Louis Horst	Isamu Noguchi	1940, Martha Graham Company
1969	Shanta Quintet	Robert Cohan	John Mayer		
1969	Cortège	BarryMoreland	J.S. Bach		
1969	Hermit Songs	Alvin Ailey	Samuel Barber		1962, Alvin Ailey Company
1969	Side Scene	Robert Cohan	Pre-classic music	Norberto Chiesa	
1969	Hosannas	Barry Moreland	Scarlatti	Richard Armstrong	
1969	Cell	Robert Cohan	Ronald Lloyd	Norberto Chiesa	
1970	Three Epitaphs	Paul Taylor	Laneville-Johnson Union Brass Band	Robert Rauschenberg	1956, Paul Taylor Company
1970	Conversation Piece	Robert North	Michael Parsons		
1970	Vasilii Icones	William Louther	Peter Maxwell Davies		
1970	Something To Do	Richard Alston	Gertrude Stein		
1971	Kontakion	Barry Moreland	Renaissance Festival, Spanish Mediaeval	Barry Moreland	
1971	Stages	Robert Cohan	Arne Nordheim/ Bob Downes	Peter Farmer	
1972	One Was The Other	Noemi Lapzeson and Robert North	Michael Finnissy	Norberto Chiesa	
1972	Relay	Siobhan Davies	Colin Wood and Bernard Watson		

Year	Title	Choreographer	Music	Design	Notes
1972	People Alone	Robert Cohan	Bob Downes	Norberto Chiesa	
1972	Outside-In	Micha Bergese and Anthony van Laast	John Lansdowne and Alan Sutcliffe		
1972	Brian	Robert North	Michael Finnissy and John Dodson	Peter Owen	
1972	Tiger Balm	Richard Alston	Anna Lockwood	Peter Farmer	
1974	Dressed To Kill	Robert North	Henry Miller and Dennis Smith		
1974	Pilot	Siobhan Davies	Igg Welthy, Stephen Barker		
1974	The Calm	Siobhan Davies	Geoffrey Burgon	Bill Gibb	
1974	Diversion of Angels	Martha Graham	Norman Dello Joio		1948, The Martha Graham Company
1974	Changing	Dan Waggoner			
1974	Troy Game	Robert North	Batacuda/Bob Downes	Peter Farmer	
1975	Class	Robert Cohan	Jon Keliehor	Charter	
1975	Masque of Separation	Robert Cohan	Burt Alcantara	Norberto Chiesa	
1975	Place of Change	Robert Cohan	Arnold Schoenberg	Charter	
1975	Diary	Sue Davies	Morris Pert	Charter	
1975	Stabat Mater	Robert Cohan	Antonio Vivaldi	Norberto Chiesa	
1976	Khamsin	Robert Cohan	Bob Downes	Norberto Chiesa	
1976	Nympheas	Micha Bergese	Claude Debussy	Bettina Bergese	
	Nema		Eberhard Schoener		
1976	Step At A Time	Siobhan Davies	Geoffrey Burgon		
1977	Rainbow Bandit	Richard Alston	Charles Armarkhanian		
1977	Sphinx	Siobhan Davies	Barrington Pheloung		
1978	Eos	Robert Cohan	Barry Guy	Barney Wan	
1978	Ice	Robert Cohan	Morton Subotnick	Norberto Chiesa	
1978	Just Before	Anthony van Laast	Anthony van Laast	Angela Hawkins	
1978	9–5	Tom Jobe	John Lewis	Paul Dart	
1978	Three Solos	Linda Gibbs	Dudley James	Jenny Henry	
1978	Sandsteps	Christopher Bannerman	Marcus West		

141

DATE OF FIRST PERFORMANCE BY L.C.D.T	TITLE	CHOREOGRAPHER	COMPOSER	DESIGNER	DATE OF FIRST PERFORMANCE IF ORIGINALLY PRODUCED ELSEWHERE
1978	Treading	Christopher Bannerman	Daniel Easterbrook		
1978	Solo Ride	Micha Bergese	Douglas Gould	Liz da Costa	
1978	Then You Can Only Sing	Siobhan Davies	Judyth Knight	Jenny Henry	
1978	Dreams With Silences	Robert North	Johannes Brahms	Norberto Chiesa	
1978	Scriabin Preludes and Studies	Robert North	Alexander Scriabin	Peter Farmer	
1979	Annunciation	Robert North	Howard Blake		
1979	Songs, Lamentations and Praises	Robert Cohan	Geoffrey Burgon	Norberto Chiesa	
1979	Rondo	Robert Cohan	John Herbert McDowell	Barney Wan	
1979	Cloven Kingdom	Paul Taylor	Henry Cowell, Malloy Miller Arcangelo Corelli	Jennifer Tipton	1976, Paul Taylor Company
1980	Death and the Maiden	Robert North	Franz Schubert		
1980	Something To Tell	Siobhan Davies	Benjamin Britten		
1980	The Singing	Christopher Bannerman	Barrington Pheloung		
1981	Dances of Love and Death	Robert Cohan	Carl Davis, Conlon Nancarrow	Norberto Chiesa	
1981	Free Setting	Siobhan Davies	Michael Finnissy	David Buckland	
1982	The Brood	Richard Kutch	Pierre Schaeffer	Francois Barbeau	1967, Batsheva Dance Company
1982	Esplanade	Paul Taylor	J.S. Bach		1975, Paul Taylor Company
1982	Chamber Dances	Robert Cohan	Geoffrey Burgon	Charter	

Chapter 5

The Scottish Ballet

Robin Anderson

The history of The Scottish Ballet falls into four periods:

Pre–1969	the origins of the company,
1969–73	the early years,
1974–78	the years of development
1979 to present day	the period of consolidation.

The origins of the company

Although The Scottish Ballet was first formed in 1969, the need for a fully professional dance company based in Scotland had been recognised for almost twenty years before.

Until then the big cities in Scotland, such as Edinburgh, Glasgow, Aberdeen and Dundee, had relied on visits from ballet companies from London. Sadler's Wells Ballet, London Festival Ballet and Ballet Rambert had all performed fairly regularly in Scotland and other now defunct companies such as Metropolitan Ballet, Ballets Russes, International Ballet and the Anglo-Polish Ballet had helped to build an audience for dance. The Edinburgh International Festival which takes place in late summer each year had also introduced many well-known dance and ballet companies from abroad to Scotland.

It began to be obvious that Scotland should have a regular performing company of its own and in the late 1950s and early 1960s several of Scotland's leading teachers of dancing formed individual small performing groups of student dancers, strengthened by guest dancers brought up from the South. The most notable of these teachers were Marjory Middleton who formed Edinburgh Ballet Club; Catherine Marks who formed Glasgow Theatre Ballet; Veronica Bruce who formed Cygnet Ballet and Glenerney Ballet Festival; and Margaret Morris who formed Celtic Ballet of Scotland and Scottish National Ballet.

All met with some degree of success, but all of them had to operate without the help of any public subsidy and so could only afford to perform at irregular intervals. Although many talented dancers developed they were forced to move South to obtain regular full-time employment and so the teacher/directors of the various small companies had to start all over again to train dancers of a sufficiently good standard.

Nevertheless it looked for a time as if a permanent dance company for Scotland might be formed from a combination of these various groups. In the middle 1960s the Scottish Arts Council began to discuss this possibility and talked to various teachers and dancers, particularly Scottish dancers who were employed with the London companies or who had worked abroad. It was realised however that much hard work would have to be done to produce a standard of performance which would even begin to compare with the visiting companies from the South.

However, this particular line of development was not to be. In

1968 the Arts Council of Great Britain produced a report on the provisions of opera and ballet in Great Britain and came to the conclusion that one of the smaller English companies might be persuaded to move north to Scotland to form a resident company there. After discussion between the Scottish Arts Council and the Arts Council of Great Britain, it was decided that Western Theatre Ballet should be invited to undertake this task.

Western Theatre Ballet
Western Theatre Ballet had been formed in 1957 with its base in Bristol. It grew out of the vision of Elizabeth West who felt that a company need not have a London home and could exist in a provincial city and have a responsibility to provide dance on a more regional basis. At the time this was a new idea, but of course it later proved to be a most important one in the development of dance and opera in Great Britain. At the present time we have several important companies with homes outside London such as The Scottish Ballet and Scottish Opera in Glasgow, Opera North in Leeds, Northern Ballet Theatre in Manchester, Welsh National Opera in Cardiff and Kent Opera in Ashford as well as a host of smaller dance companies throughtout the country.

In 1957 Elizabeth West had been working at Bristol's Old Vic Theatre and she became convinced that a small dance company could be based there with special responsibilities for touring the smaller towns in the West Country. She invited Peter Darrell to join her in running the company and to become resident chor-eographer of the new group. Peter Darrell had trained at the Sadler's Wells Ballet School, now The Royal Ballet School, at the same time as Kenneth MacMillan who is now resident chor-eographer of The Royal Ballet and John Cranko who became director of the Stuttgart Ballet in Germany. He had danced with Sadler's Wells Ballet, London Festival Ballet and with companies in Paris and had choreographed one of television's first pop music shows called *Cool for Cats*. His choreographic work for Ballet Workshop in London had caused much interest and he seemed to have the breadth of experience which Elizabeth West felt was necessary for the new company.

Both West and Darrell felt that ballet need not necessarily have an exclusive image of sylphs in pretty dresses, pink tights and pointe shoes, but could deal also with modern themes and con-temporary problems. As the company gained in strength and reputation, Darrell became joint director and he and Elizabeth West continued to run the company. The partnership ended with

145

Elizabeth West's untimely death on holiday when she was killed in an avalance while searching for alpine flowers.

From 1957 to 1964 the company performed in small theatres in England, particularly in the West Country, and toured abroad to Italy, Belgium and the United States. It also appeared in pantomime and revue. In 1965 Western Theatre Ballet decided to forsake its first principle and move to London to become associated with Sadler's Wells Opera, now the English National Opera at Sadler's Wells Theatre. Peter Darrell was responsible for the artistic direction of the opera ballet, both in London and on tour. The association with Sadler's Wells Opera gave Western Theatre Ballet the opportunity to use more dancers, and to stage longer and more ambitious ballets.

However, the link-up between opera and ballet brought problems. Too often the dancer is merely seen to be a 'spear carrier' to fill up the crowd scenes in opera, and so Western Theatre Ballet often found itself having to curtail its own tours to fit in with the opera performance schedule.

So it was, that in 1969, Western Theatre Ballet with Peter Darrell as its artistic director decided to accept the invitation of the Scottish Arts Council to form the beginnings of a resident ballet company for Scotland.

Northern Ballet Theatre

At the same time, the associate director, Laverne Meyer, went to Manchester with some of the dancers to form the beginning of a new regional company called Northern Dance Theatre, now Northern Ballet Theatre. Thus Western Theatre Ballet has the distinction of having been the parent of the two major regionally based Arts Council supported dance companies in the United Kingdom.

Scottish Theatre Ballet

In Scotland, the new company was called Scottish Theatre Ballet and gave its first performance at Perth on 9 April 1969. This arrangement of bringing a major part of an existing company to Scotland had the great advantage that it could begin performing immediately. Here was a group of dancers and staff who were used to working with each other and the company already had a repertoire of exciting ballets. The alternative idea of setting up a company from scratch would have meant a delay of at least six months to a year while dancers were auditioned, and staff were recruited and an even longer period of perhaps two or three years until the same standards of performance were achieved.

1969–73; the early years

The original idea was that Scottish Theatre Ballet could work closely with Scottish Opera which had been formed in 1962 and was already well established. Accordingly one floor of Scottish Opera's headquarters was set aside for the ballet's exclusive use giving two dance studios, a green-room, a small office and primitive changing rooms. In view of the company's problems at Sadler's Wells, a policy was evolved which gave the ballet company a completely different and entirely separate management. However it still provided for the opportunity to collaborate with Scottish Opera on major productions where dance formed an important part of the overall production.

Continuity was preserved through Peter Darrell as artistic director and Muriel Large as administrator, both of whom had been responsible for the company after Elizabeth West's death. They were accompanied by some of the original dancers such as Elaine McDonald, Sally Collard-Gentle, Robin Haig, Patricia Rianne, Bronwen Curry, Susan Carlton, Brian Burn, Peter Cazalet, Terence James, Domy Reiter and Kenn Wells. The training of the dancers and rehearsals were in the hands of Gordon Aitken and Harry Haythorne.

That this was a highly talented group can be demonstrated by the subsequent careers of these people. Elaine McDonald is now principal ballerina of The Scottish Ballet and is recognised as one of Europe's notable ballerinas. Peter Darrell is still artistic director and has transformed the company into one of international repute; Sally Collard-Gentle, after a spell as soloist with the Australian Ballet, returned as a principal dancer of The Scottish Ballet; Robin Haig became artistic director of the West Australian Ballet and now teaches in America; Patricia Rianne has danced with many other companies and has recently staged ballets for the New Zealand Ballet; Bronwen Curry is recognised as one of the leading dance notators of the Benesh system; Susan Carlton has done much work with young dancers in Singapore; Peter Cazalet is now one of South Africa's leading theatrical designers; Terence James was principal teacher of Scottish Ballet's school; Domy Reiter is principal choreographer for the Irish Ballet Company; Kenn Wells is a principal dancer with London Festival Ballet; Gordon Aitken is assistant director of The Scottish Ballet and Harry Haythorne was artistic director of the Queensland Ballet in Australia before becoming artistic director of The Royal New Zealand Ballet.

The first big production for the company was *Beauty and the Beast*, a new full-length ballet choreographed by Darrell in 1969 to a specially commissioned score by Thea Musgrave. The repertoire also had shorter ballets by Jack Carter, Flemming Flindt, Clover Roope, Gillian Lynne and John Neumeier all of whom had international reputations as choreographers. The one ballet in that first season which had a distinctly classical history was August Bournonville's *La Ventana* which had been first produced in 1854.

Bournonville (1805–79) was a very famous ballet master of the Royal Danish Ballet in Copenhagen in the nineteenth century and his work has had a very considerable influence on the history of ballet since. The style of dancing is a very pure one and his system of teaching has been handed down from generation to generation of teachers and dancers in Copenhagen. The decision to mount *La Ventana* was one which was to have long-term effects in the development of The Scottish Ballet.

Almost from the beginning three very important activities were undertaken in addition to the main performances in the major cities and theatres in Scotland. The first was the establishment of periodic choreographic workshops where, in less formal surroundings, young choreographers could gain experience in their craft. Although in the initial stages some of the choreographers came from outside, most were dancing members of the company who were choreographing for the first time.

Secondly it was realised that if the new company was to become an important part of the cultural life of Scotland it should be seen not only in the main cities and theatres, but also in the smaller towns and communities throughout Scotland. Therefore the repertoire would consist of more modest ballets which were suitable for these less well-equipped stages. The important thought behind these performances was that although smaller in scale, they should involve the company's best dancers and have the best possible standards of costume, lighting and presentation.

Finally special consideration was to be given to the interests of young people. Stuart Hopps arrived to take charge of these activities and set about making contacts with teachers in schools, and lecturers in colleges and universities. Soon things had advanced to a stage when he could engage an assistant to work with him and The Scottish Ballet's Moveable Workshop was launched to work in schools throughout Scotland and to introduce the experience of dance and movement to young people.

The year 1970 continued with new short ballets such as *Dances from William Tell,* a second Bournonville work. However the major effort was an entirely new production of *Giselle* by Peter Darrell. *Giselle* is possibly the best known and most popular of the romantic ballets and was first produced in Paris in 1841. Since then it has featured in the repertoire of almost every major classical ballet company in the world.

In the Scottish Theatre Ballet version, although nearly all of what is believed to be the original choreography is incorporated, the theme of the ballet is set in an earlier period and the situation of the first act has been changed to a small village square. This seemed to make more sense of the idea of medieval superstition which is important to the plot and is the reason for Giselle's suicide. Although Peter Darrell gave the ballet these new slants he based his version on the original score by Adolphe Adam. This was contrary to what had often happened, since almost from the beginning of that ballet's life additional and often unsuitable music had been included to provide extra dances or to show off a particular dancer's talents. This was not an uncommon practice in the nineteenth century.

The success of *Giselle* in the repertoire suggested that the company was now ready to take on the role of a national ballet for Scotland and gave Peter Darrell the confidence to mount an entirely new full-length ballet for the company called *Tales of Hoffmann* in 1972.

Tales of Hoffmann had existed as a famous opera for almost a century, with a good story and a tuneful score. In it, Hoffmann tells three stories of his ill-fated love affairs with a magic doll, a courtesan and finally an opera singer. In his ballet Darrell made the obvious and necessary alteration of changing one of the heroines from an opera singer to a ballerina, and also changed the order of the second and third tales, keeping the one he felt offered the most exciting dance possibilities to the last. This ballet with the score of Jacques Offenbach's music skillfully rearranged by John Lanchbery proved to be an instant success and is still a popular item in the company's repertoire. Although a completely new ballet, it was constructed on the lines of the late nineteenth-century classics and fitted in well with the company's idea of developing a repertoire of established classics while still preserving strongly dramatic ideas and themes.

It was perhaps inevitable that the company should next try to produce one of the great classics and *The Nutcracker* seemed an obvious choice. This ballet, which had been first produced in St.

Petersburg in Russia, has as its main theme a children's Christmas party. Little Clara, the daughter of the house, falls asleep and in her dreams travels through the realm of ice and snow to the kingdom of the sweets in the company of the Nutcracker Prince. The prince was transformed in Clara's dream from one of her Christmas gifts, a huge nutcracker in the shape of a soldier doll.

In The Scottish Ballet version Peter Darrell decided to use real children for all the young parts. Usually Clara and her brother Fritz are danced by adults. The new version was first performed in its entirety during Christmas 1973 although the second act with its many *divertissements* had been performed as part of a triple bill on tour earlier that year. It was another success and has been performed by The Scottish Ballet almost every Christmas since then. Although the ballet uses the original Tchaikovsky score, Darrell's retelling of the story required new choreography throughout and the only part which uses the original Ivanov choreography is the grand *pas de deux* for the Sugar Plum Fairy and the Nutcracker Prince in the last act.

1973 also saw the première of another major work which was almost to become the company's trademark. As we have seen, the repertoire already included two short ballets by August Bournonville. One of this choreographer's best-known works was *La Sylphide*, originally choreographed in 1836 and continually in the repertoire of the Royal Danish Ballet to the present day. It was an obvious choice for Scottish Theatre Ballet since the original story was set in Scotland and concerned a young laird's infatuation for a woodland sprite, the sylphide of the title. The Scots brought a sense of realism and authenticity to the ballet with its setting of a large Scottish country farmhouse, the traditional costume of the kilt for the men and the exciting reels and balletic interpretations of Scottish folk dancing.

During the early period of the company a start was also made in helping with the training of young Scottish dancers, whom it was hoped might provide future professional dancers for the company. Accordingly private dance teachers in Central Scotland were invited to send promising young students for audition with the idea that if any interesting talent was found Scottish Theatre Ballet would provide free scholarship classes at the week-end to supplement the teaching of the student's own dance teacher. Although it was realised that this was not a very satisfactory scheme and in no way offered the same standard of training as schools such as the Royal Ballet school it was the best that could be done at the time.

Nevertheless the scheme did produce some talented dancers who, in direct competition to those trained at schools in England, did make the grade and by 1981 the company had one principal dancer, two soloists and one coryphée whose only training was by the scholarship system.

By the beginning of 1974 Scottish Theatre Ballet had grown from its original eighteen dancers to a company of twenty-eight and the orchestra, originally only sixteen strong which accompanied the first performance of *Giselle*, was extended to thirty-five. The style of the company had also changed, no longer did the ballets tend only to be short ones with modern themes, but a greater emphasis was placed on full-length classical ballets.

Indeed from this account it might seem that the company's new works were entirely full-length classics, but a detailed investigation would show that almost forty new one-act ballets were presented during the period 1969 to 1974. Nevertheless the significant achievement during this period was the development of the company from a small group to a company which was beginning to show encouraging signs of fulfilling a national duty. The full-length ballets were an important step in achieving this aim.

1974–78: the years of development

Scottish Theatre Ballet was now firmly poised to achieve its goal of being recognised as a major dance company in Great Britain. It had certainly begun to be accepted in Scotland. The company which had arrived as 'foreigners' five years before was steadily being recognised as part of the general cultural scene. The original board of directors from Bristol and London had steadily been replaced by directors resident in Scotland and this transfer was finally completed in 1973 when Ann Hewer J.P. who had been chairman of the board throughout the Western Theatre Ballet days resigned in favour of Robin Duff who is currently president.

At the same time the administrator Muriel Large left to take up the position of administrator of the Irish Ballet Company based in Cork. In her place, the board appointed Robin Anderson, a Scot who had been administrator of Harrogate Theatre and manager of the Leicester Phoenix Theatre. A pharmaceutical chemist and former ice-skating champion of Scotland, he had been involved with some of the earlier attempts to form a dance company in Scotland before undertaking an Arts Council administration training scheme. With a Scottish board of directors and a Scottish administrator the company was now well able to strengthen its presence in Scotland.

Darrell and Anderson realised that a real acceptance of the company in Scotland as a national asset would depend on the recognition of the company's quality outside its native country. Whilst the company had toured in England for three or four weeks each year since it was formed, it had not yet returned to London since the first season as Scottish Theatre Ballet and, importantly, had not appeared abroad.

The chance to achieve the second of these ambitions came in 1974 when an eight-week tour of Australia and New Zealand was offered. However, the impressario who made the offer set the condition that the company must be accompanied by two guest star dancers of international fame. It had been suggested that *La Sylphide* should be the major ballet of the tour and, knowing that she had never danced the role, Darrell offered the part to Dame Margot Fonteyn. To the company's relief she accepted and she was joined by Ivan Nagy, a Hungarian dancer who had defected to the west, had become an Australian citizen and was now one of the leading dancers of American Ballet Theatre in New York.

The company flew out in the spring of 1974 to open its tour at

Perth in Western Australia. As was appropriate to the new look of the company the opportunity was taken to shorten the official name to The Scottish Ballet. The company danced in Perth, Melbourne, Adelaide, and Sydney in Australia and in Wellington and Dunedin in New Zealand. It returned to Scotland that summer to find it had achieved a measure of international recognition.

In the following year, 1975, further tours abroad took place, to the International Festival of Dance in Madrid with Rudolf Nureyev and in the Festival of Barcelona. It was not until 1976 that the company returned to London to appear at Sadler's Wells Theatre. In an ambitious programme it presented amongst others new to the capital, two of Peter Darrell's newest ballets.

The Scarlet Pastorale had been premièred the previous autumn in Scotland. It was an extended one-act ballet whose theme was based on the famous Aubrey Beardsley drawings. The designer Philip Prowse had brilliantly transposed Beardsley's fantastic costumes to a reality on stage. *Mary, Queen of Scots* took on the somewhat difficult task of telling the dramatic story of Scotland's tragic Queen from her childhood days at the French court to her death by beheading at Fotheringhay by order of Queen Elizabeth I. It was too complicated a plot to be successful as a ballet, but did, particularly in the final scenes, give Elaine McDonald some marvellous opportunities to show the dramatic intensity of her dancing.

Almost the next engagement for the company was a return visit to London to dance in Rudolf Nureyev's season at the London Coliseum in the summer of 1976. The performance of *La Sylphide* was almost abandoned one night when Nureyev injured himself. However, Graham Bart, one of The Scottish Ballet's own dancers, took over the role for the second act and although the audience were disappointed in not seeing Nureyev, gave Bart a rousing welcome. It was a measure of the company's strength that out of an audience of well over 2,000 people only six asked for their money back.

The next big classical ballet to be attempted was Darrell's version of *Swan Lake*, the three-act ballet to Tchaikovsky's music. This is probably the best-known ballet in the dance repertoire and The Scottish Ballet version made the hero an opium-smoking prince, who sees the enchanted lake and swans through his drugged dreams. This concept scandalised some of the ballet purists but gave a perfectly valid interpretation of the story. Such are the conventions of the present times that the opium dreams of

Vespri, a suite of dances to music by Verdi, choreographed by André Prokovsky, which has been a popular feature of the repertoire first performed in 1977. Photo: William Cooper.

Arabian Nights could be thought quite charming in Victorian days whereas the same idea upset some members of a modern audience.

Later in 1977 the company returned to Spain and France to dance in San Sebastian, Biarritz and St. Jean de Luz. But The Scottish Ballet's work at home in Scotland did not diminish. A spring and autumn tour of the big Scottish theatres took place every year and the small-scale Ballet for Scotland tours continued to range from Wick and Thurso in the north to Dumfries and Galashiels in the south. New one-act ballets entered the repertoire with choreography by Toer van Schayk, Fokine, Darrell, Carter, Gore, Petipa, Béjart, Dolin and Murray Louis, and yearly workshop performances gave many young choreographers the chance to develop their work.

Meanwhile on the educational side Stuart Hopps continued to develop the work with young people and the Moveable Workshop grew to five dancers, a musician and a technician. It began to give performances in schools as well as giving young people the chance to dance themselves. However in 1974 Stuart Hopps decided to leave to take up a career as a free-lance choreographer and the position of director of the Workshop was taken by Sue Weston. With what was initially a smaller group, she carried on the work in the same pattern and also arranged several presentations which linked the work done by school pupils in dance classes with those in sport on the playing field.

The scholarship ballet classes also continued and even younger pupils were auditioned and enrolled to give them the benefit of a longer period of training. An important development at this time was obtaining the permission of Equity, the dancers' trade union, to take two of the talented scholars into the company each year as dance apprentices to see if their classroom talent would develop in the more difficult conditions of a professional ballet company.

The achievements of this second stage in the life of The Scottish Ballet had not, perhaps, the pioneering flavour of the earlier periods. However it had grown again in size. By 1978 the company consisted of forty-two dancers, eight technical staff and an administration staff of twelve. When the company appeared in the main theatres the orchestra consisted of forty-five players and, whereas in the earlier years the orchestra had been begged or borrowed from other organisations, there was now a Scottish Ballet Orchestra.

Although the Scottish Arts Council had proved sympathetic to the development plans of the company it was seldom to provide the full amount of cash required. The fact that the repertoire had many popular ballets ensured that money paid by the public for theatre tickets increased year by year. This together with a new strict control of expenses made sure that in spite of the increased costs of running the company it was always able to survive financially.

1979–: the period of consolidation

As has been seen, for the first nine years of its life The Scottish Ballet shared rehearsal premises with Scottish Opera, but the company had long outgrown the available space. The administrative, publicity and financial offices had moved to rented accommodation half a mile away. The wardrobe department was housed in basement premises near by and the scenery and costume stocks were stored fifty miles away in Edinburgh.

After several years of search, during which it was at one time thought the company might move its base to Edinburgh, an almost derelict property in the West End of Glasgow was found. Formerly a Territorial Army headquarters, the building offered great potential for the very specialised requirements of a ballet company. It could provide extensive office accommodation for the various departments necessary in running a company of this size, but most importantly it would have several large areas capable of being made into rehearsal studios. The property was purchased for £30,000 and the company set about finding the other £200,000 that would be required to pay for the costs of converting and equipping the building for its new role. In 1978 a public appeal was launched and eighteen months later nearly a quarter of a million pounds had been gathered from private donations, business organisations, local authorities and the Arts Council.

In March 1979, to celebrate the tenth birthday of The Scottish Ballet, Her Majesty, Queen Elizabeth, The Queen Mother performed the official opening ceremony. The premises provided under one roof, three large dance studios, a smaller practice room, an attractively furnished green-room for the dancers, changing rooms equipped with showers, a music library, wardrobe and spacious office accommodation. The studios all had specially sprung wooden floors and were equipped with pianos and tape recorders as well as facilities for video recording and play-back.

These new headquarters gave the company a permanent home of its own and a firmer base for its tours throughout Scotland. It also gave the opportunity for more experimental and creative work. To do this, one of the studios was capable of being transformed into a small performing area with room for an audience of

The Scottish Ballet's prima ballerina Elaine McDonald dances Terasina's solo in the last act of Napoli.
Photo: William Cooper.

fifty people. At least twice each year since the headquarters were opened, a series of evenings of experimental ballet have been given with dances choreographed by younger dance members of the company. Two of them, Garry Trinder and Peter Royston, have since choreographed works for major tours by The Scottish Ballet. Their work showed real promise and was well received by the critics.

New works for the company were not neglected. 1978 saw the acquisition of another full-length Bournonville ballet. This was *Napoli*, and The Scottish Ballet became the first British company ever to stage this work. Indeed The Scottish Ballet now had the biggest repertoire of Bournonville ballets of any company outside Denmark. *Napoli* is set on a quayside in Naples and is a simple tale of the love of a young fisherman for Terasina, the heroine of the ballet who is later shipwrecked in a storm and captured by the King of the Grotto. Gennaro, the fisherman, rescues her and the last act of the ballet is concerned with the betrothal celebrations of the young couple and is a continuous parade of most exciting dances.

During the Christmas season of 1979 a new production of *Cinderella* was created for the company by Peter Darrell. This followed the well-known pantomime story and was set to a special arrangement of most of the music by Rossini written for his opera *La Cenerentola*. This ballet has been enormously successful and has appeared each Christmas season since. These popular seasons of this ballet and *The Nutcracker* have been largely responsible for bringing a new audience, particularly of young people, into the theatre who might not, in the usual course of events, have attended ballet performances. Many have discovered in this way that ballet is something to be enjoyed and have returned to see other performances of classical and modern ballets at other times of the year, so enlarging the company's regular audience.

1979 was also remarkable in the presentation of three new ballets danced under the single title of *Underground Rumours*. For this the company went to two young musicians not usually noted for composing music for ballet. These were Jon Anderson of the modern group 'Yes', and Ian Anderson, the leader of the rock group 'Jethro Tull', who composed new scores for two of the ballets, *Ursprung* choreographed by Royston Maldoom and *The Water's Edge* choreographed by Robert North. The third ballet of this triple bill was *Such Sweet Thunder* to Duke Ellington's music of the same title. This was a light-hearted musical interpretation of

The Mermaids from Robert North's ballet The Water's Edge, *originally performed as one of three ballets in* Underground Rumours.
Photo: William Cooper

some of Shakespeare's best known heroes and heroines. In the ballet, Peter Darrell carried the joke still further by getting the dancers to perform imitations of how great Hollywood screen actors and actresses would have interpreted the roles. Thus Cleopatra became Claudette Colbert: Lady Macbeth was Rita Hayworth and Romeo and Juliet were Marlon Brando and Natalie Wood.

In 1980, although recession made things difficult financially, the company was able to present a new ballet, *Cheri*, when it was invited to dance for a second time at the Edinburgh International Festival. *Cheri* was another new Darrell ballet which was based on the classic French novel of the same name by Colette. In this, Peter Darrell was lucky to have the assistance of Colette's daughter, Colette de Jouvenal, in preparing the scenario. The music was specially composed by a young South African musician, David Earl.

The major new ballet in 1981 was *Symphony in D* by Czechoslovakian choreographer Jiri Kylian, artistic director of Nederlands Dans Theater. He is one of the most sought-after choreographers in the world today. In acquiring this work, The Scottish Ballet scored another success, being the first British company to have a new work by Kylian in its repertoire.

The summer of 1981 also had some interesting tours abroad. In June the company travelled to Venice to take part in the International Festival of Dance and, amongst the fifteen companies participating, was the only major ballet company. The Scottish Ballet's performances were given in the magnificent Teatro La Fenice and the programmes consisted of *Napoli* and a triple bill of *Jeux* and *Othello*, both by Darrell, and Jack Carter's exciting *Three Dances to Japanese Music*. The visit was a great success, although the Italian audiences were a little uncertain of *Napoli* which is a sketch of Neapolitan fisher folk as seen through the eyes of a nineteenth-century Dane and danced by twentieth-century Scots! In the Autumn of 1981 the company also returned to Spain to dance in Santander and San Sebastian and to France to Biarritz and St. Jean de Luz.

Cheri, *Peter Darrell's choreographic interpretation of the novel by Colette, which was first performed during the Edinburgh International Festival in 1980.*
Photo: William Cooper.

An exciting moment from Three Dances to Japanese Music *which was created for The Scottish Ballet by Jack Carter in 1973 when they appeared at the Edinburgh Festival.*
Photo: William Cooper.

In the 1982 Spring tour the company premièred a new full-length production. This was the first staging by a British company of John Cranko's *Romeo and Juliet*. Cranko had first made this work for the Milan ballet company in 1958 and had reworked it in a final version for his own company, the Stuttgart Ballet, in 1962. John Cranko had died tragically of a heart attack in 1973. He had been a fellow student of Peter Darrell at Sadler's Wells Ballet School in the late 1940s. Both had developed similar choreographic beliefs. The sets and costumes were by Jurgen Rose, the original designer.

In 1983 two new works were first danced and formed part of a programme of ballets to music by Frederick Chopin. The performance commenced with Fokine's great classic *Les Sylphides* and this was followed by *Quarrels not their Own*, a commissioned work by a young dancer in the company, Peter Royston. He had attracted attention with his work for some of the experimental studio programmes and one of his pieces had been performed in the main tours; he was now given the opportunity to create specifically for this purpose. The ballet spanned a period covering the reigns of George V, George VI and Elizabeth II and showed in the first episode a young couple's early married bliss, in the second the husband's death in World War II, and finally, in the last part, the now old woman dreaming of the memory of her lost love. The ballet had an ingenious setting on two levels designed by a young Glasgow artist Kenny McLellan. The second of the two new works was by Peter Darrell, called *Gardens of the Night,* in which he explored the relationship between Chopin and the lady novelist George Sand as well as other literary figures from the early part of the twentieth century such as Virginia Woolf and Vita Sackville-West.

In 1983 The Scottish Ballet gave the greatest number of performances abroad ever achieved by the company, dancing in Lisbon, Oporto, Granada, Istanbul, Cyprus, Athens, Amman and Qatar.

During this period a change in policy in the Workshop group also occurred. The steady development of dance in schools, mainly in physical education departments, meant that The Scottish Ballet's Workshop group no longer had the same pioneering responsibilities. Of course the presence of dance in schools was not uniform, but where it did exist the education authorities were less anxious to pay for a service from outside. Equally, The Scottish Ballet, in increasingly difficult financial times, could no longer afford to continue to provide these services free. Discussions took place and it was decided to make certain policy changes. Sue Weston, the director, felt that she did not want to alter the work and structure of the group which she had built so she resigned and Ann Baird was appointed as director of young people's activities.

Although not a dancer herself, Ann Baird had been instrumental in evolving an Opera for Youth programme for Scottish Opera which had been presented with great success and involved the participation of school pupils in performances of their own.

Scottish Ballet Steps Out

A new group, The Scottish Ballet Steps Out, was formed in 1981 and consisted of three teacher/dancers whose task was to act as pioneers in schools where dance did not form part of the physical education syllabus. In schools where dance already existed within the timetable they would provide an additional stimulus and expertise for the benefit of pupils and teachers alike. The initial contact was backed up by a new activity when performances of

David Bombana as Romeo watches the duel between Mercutio (Vincent Hantam) and Tybalt (Jonathan Kelly) in The Scottish Ballet's production of John Cranko's Romeo and Juliet.
Photo: Antonia Reeve.

ballets in schools were given by members of the main Scottish Ballet company. In this way the company hoped to achieve a link and continuity between dance as part of education and dance as a theatre performance.

Vocational Dance Education Scheme
This last period also saw developments of The Scottish Ballet's Vocational Dance Education Scheme. It was mentioned earlier that when the company first came to Scotland efforts were made to provide additional tuition for pupils already attending classes given by private teachers of dance. Although many present members of the company came through this system it had always been recognised that a higher concentration of training was required to produce a dancer with as wide a range of expertise as could be gained by attendance at full-time dance-training schools such as

the Royal Ballet School and the Arts Educational School. With financial assistance from the Strathclyde Regional Local Authority a new system was set up in 1979 whereby children from nine years onward could receive free tuition twice a week through to the age of fifteen and three times a week between fifteen and seventeen.

A further development occurred in the early part of 1982 when Strathclyde Region Education Department announced it would set up a dance education unit in association with The Scottish Ballet at an existing secondary comprehensive school in Glasgow. Under these plans children resident in Strathclyde who showed a real talent for dance would be able to attend that school for a full dance education as well as a normal education leading to 'O' and 'A' levels in general academic subjects. This would exist within the normal state education scheme and would be available at no cost to the parents.

By autumn 1983, the dance education unit was established at Knightswood School in the West End of Glasgow where a surplus gymnasium was turned into a large dance studio and additional classroom space was provided. With the stated intention of Strathclyde Region Education Department to make the unit a national facility, the close proximity of residential hostel accommodation as well as the nearness to The Scottish Ballet's own studios were important deciding factors in the choice of school.

It is doubtful if The Scottish Ballet will ever consist entirely of dancers trained in its own school. Dance is an art form that has no language barrier and the multi-national aspects of a ballet company are a strength. The Scottish Ballet has dancers from Australia, South Africa, Portugal, Japan and Singapore as well as English and Scottish dancers.

Still expanding in 1982, The Scottish Ballet purchased two large derelict buildings at the rear of its present headquarters and announced its intention to develop these to provide a studio/theatre to seat about 200 people together with a large area to store the huge collection of scenery and costumes. By the end of 1983, the first phase of this scheme was completed, leaving only the studio theatre to be fully equipped as money became available from the public appeal for funds to pay for the project.

The Scottish Ballet is now recognised as a national ballet with an international reputation, having earned this status through its wide range of performing activities at home and abroad, its educational activities, the formation of its own school and its own headquarters. The fact that this has been achieved in a little over ten years is ample demonstration of the need for such a company in Scotland and is a forceful example of the importance of dance within the whole range of the performing arts.

Suggested further reading

Dixon, J.S. (1981) *Elaine McDonald*, Leeds: Arno.
Goodwin, N. (1979) *A ballet for Scotland*, Edinburgh: Canongate Publishing.
Scottish Ballet Magazine 1978–83, Glasgow: The Scottish Ballet.

The Scottish Ballet:
chart showing significant events in the history of the company.

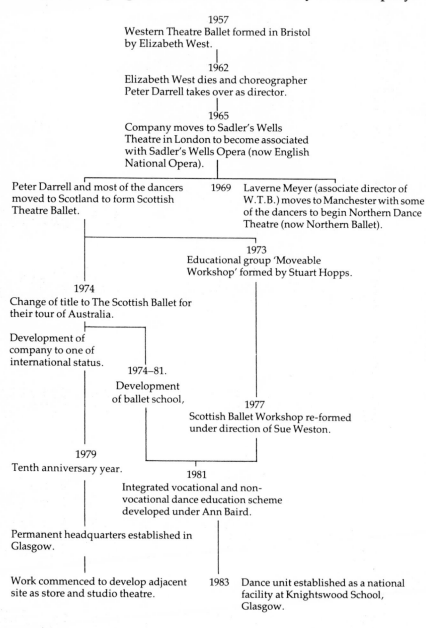

1957
Western Theatre Ballet formed in Bristol
by Elizabeth West.

1962
Elizabeth West dies and choreographer
Peter Darrell takes over as director.

1965
Company moves to Sadler's Wells
Theatre in London to become associated
with Sadler's Wells Opera (now English
National Opera).

Peter Darrell and most of the dancers
moved to Scotland to form Scottish
Theatre Ballet.

1969   Laverne Meyer (associate director of
W.T.B.) moves to Manchester with some
of the dancers to begin Northern Dance
Theatre (now Northern Ballet).

1973
Educational group 'Moveable
Workshop' formed by Stuart Hopps.

1974
Change of title to The Scottish Ballet for
their tour of Australia.

Development of
company to one of
international status.

1974–81.
Development
of ballet school,

1977
Scottish Ballet Workshop re-formed
under direction of Sue Weston.

1979
Tenth anniversary year.

1981
Integrated vocational and non-
vocational dance education scheme
developed under Ann Baird.

Permanent headquarters established in
Glasgow.

Work commenced to develop adjacent
site as store and studio theatre.

1983   Dance unit established as a national
facility at Knightswood School,
Glasgow.

The Scottish Ballet: choreochronicle of works mentioned in the chapter

DATE OF FIRST PERFORMANCE BY THE SCOTTISH BALLET	TITLE	CHOREOGRAPHER	COMPOSER	DESIGNER	DATE OF FIRST PERFORMANCE IF ORIGINALLY PRODUCED ELSEWHERE
1969	Beauty and the Beast	Darrell	Musgrave	Docherty	
1970	Dances from William Tell	Bournonville	Rossini	Stone	1842, Royal Danish Ballet, Copenhagen.
1971	Giselle	Coralli/Perrot	Adam	Cazalet	1841, Paris Opéra.
1972	Tales of Hoffmann	Darrell	Offenbach	Livingstone	
1973	Jeux	Darrell	Debussy	Waistnage	1963, Western Theatre Ballet, Glasgow.
1973	The Nutcracker	Ivanov/Darrell	Tchaikovsky	Prowse	1892, Imperial Russian Ballet, St. Petersburg.
1973	La Sylphide	Bournonville	Lovenskjold	Cazalet	1836, Royal Danish Ballet, Copenhagen.
1973	Three Dances to Japanese Music	Carter	Trad/Katoda	McDowell	
1975	The Scarlet Pastorale	Darrell	Martin	Prowse	
1976	Mary, Queen of Scots	Darrell	McCabe	Docherty	
1976	Othello	Darrell	Liszt	Farmer	1971, New London Ballet, Trieste, Italy.
1977	Swan Lake	Petipa/Ivanov/Darrell	Tchaikovsky	Cazalet	1895, Imperial Russian Ballet, St. Petersburg.
1977	Vespri	Prokovsky	Verdi	McDowell	1973, New London Ballet, La Coruña, Spain.
1978	Napoli	Bournonville	Pauli/Helsted/Gade/Lumbye	Cazalet	1842, Royal Danish Ballet, Copenhagen.
1979	Cinderella	Darrell	Rossini	Fraser	
1979	Ursprung	Maldoom	Anderson	Bowers	
1979	The Water's Edge	North	Anderson/Palmer/Barre	Farmer	
1979	Such Sweet Thunder	Darrell	Ellington	Ringwood	
1980	Cheri	Darrell	Earl	Prowse	
1981	Symphony in D	Kylian	Haydn	Schenk	1976, Nederlands Dance Theatre
1982	Romeo and Juliet	Cranko	Prokofiev	Rose	1962, Stuttgart Ballet
1983	Quarrels not their Own	Royston	Chopin	McLellan	
1983	Les Sylphides	Fokine	Chopin	Cazalet	1909, Diaghiev Ballets Russes
1983	Gardens of the Night	Darrell	Chopin	Darrell	

Sample Examination Questions

Ballet Rambert

1. Describe the ways in which Marie Rambert has contributed to the development of dance in Britain.
2. Describe the origins and development of Ballet Rambert from 1920 to 1966. Include mention of personalities, policies and achievements.
3. The Mercury Theatre has been called the cradle of British ballet. Identify *three* people of importance who danced on its tiny stage and explain how they helped the development of British ballet.
4. Write a short paragraph on *three* of the following:
   (a) the Mercury Theatre,
   (b) the Ballet Club,
   (c) the Ballet Workshop,
   (d) the Rambert Dance Unit,
   (e) the Mercury Ensemble.
5. Explain why Norman Morrice is a person of great significance to the development of Ballet Rambert and describe the policies for which he was responsible.

The Royal Ballet and Sadler's Wells Royal Ballet

1. Describe the formation and early development of The Royal Ballet under the directorship of Ninette de Valois.
2. Write a short paragraph on *three* of the following:
   (a) the Academy of Choreographic Art,
   (b) the Camargo Society,
   (c) the Vic-Wells Ballet,
   (d) Ballet for All,
   (e) Sadler's Wells Theatre Ballet,
   (f) the New Group.

3. Write a short paragraph on *four* of the following:
   (a) Alicia Markova,
   (b) Constant Lambert,
   (c) Robert Helpmann,
   (d) Rudolf Nureyev,
   (e) Eric Bruhn,
   (f) Bronislava Nijinska,
   (g) Antony Tudor,
   (h) John Cranko.
4. Describe the role played by Sadler's Wells Ballet during the years 1939–45 and explain how their activities helped to build audiences for ballet in Britain.
5. Describe the contribution of Frederick Ashton to the development of The Royal Ballet.

London Festival Ballet

1. Write a short paragraph on *four* of the following explaining how they contributed to the development of London Festival Ballet:
   (a) Dr Julian Braunsweg,
   (b) Anton Dolin,
   (c) Alicia Markova,
   (d) John Gilpin,
   (e) Donald Albery,
   (f) John Field.
2. Describe the policies and achievements of London Festival Ballet under the directorship of Beryl Grey.
3. Describe briefly the backgrounds of Anton Dolin and Alicia Markova and explain why a knowledge of these may have influenced Dr Julian Braunsweg in his decision to invite them to be the first artistic directors of London Festival Ballet.
4. Choose any *two* ballets that London Festival Ballet has inherited from the Diaghilev repertoire. Briefly describe the ballets identifying the choreographer, composer and designer.
5. When he became director of London Festival Ballet in 1979, John Field initially decided to maintain a balance of classical, romantic and contemporary ballets. Describe *one* ballet which is representative of each of these categories. Give details of the choreographer, composer and designer.

London Contemporary Dance Theatre

1. Describe the role played by Robin Howard in the development of London Contemporary Dance Theatre.
2. Explain the contribution of Robert Cohan to the development of London Contemporary Dance Theatre.
3. Write a short paragraph on *four* of the following:
   (a) Jane Dudley,
   (b) William Louther,
   (c) Robert North
   (d) Richard Alston,
   (e) Siobhan Davies,
   (f) Micha Bergese.
4. Briefly describe the following dances and explain how they have contributed to the development of dance in Britain?
   (a) *Stages,*
   (b) *Troy Game,*
   (c) *Khamsin.*
5. What is a residency? Explain how residencies may increase knowledge of dance.

The Scottish Ballet

1. Describe the development of Western Theatre Ballet and explain its importance to the development of The Scottish Ballet.
2. Describe the ways in which The Scottish Ballet has explicitly tried to consider the interests of young people.
3. Explain the importance of the Bournonville ballets to The Scottish Ballet.
4. Describe the contribution of Peter Darrell to the development of The Scottish Ballet.
5. In choreographing his version of well-known ballets Peter Darrell often adapts the story. Choose *two* of the following ballets and describe how Darrell has modified the story of each:
   (a) *Giselle,*
   (b) *The Nutcracker,*
   (c) *Swan Lake.*

Appendix 2

Information on the Companies

Ballet Rambert

Ballet Rambert is based in Chiswick, West London, in a converted furniture store. In this building are two rehearsal studios, the administrative offices and the wardrobe and workshop areas where costumes and sets are made. The address is:

Ballet Rambert
94 Chiswick High Road
London W4 1SH
Telephone: 01-995 4246

Ballet Rambert performs in London mainly at Sadler's Wells Theatre and tours to medium and large-scale theatres throughout Britain. The company also tours abroad once or twice each year. For details of performances please contact the Press and Public Relations officer. For information on Ballet Rambert's education activities and teaching resource materials please contact the Education Liaison Officer.

The Royal Ballet and Sadler's Wells Royal Ballet

The Royal Ballet is the resident ballet company at the Royal Opera House, Covent Garden, where it shares seasons, from September/October – July/August, with The Royal Opera. The company sometimes performs in the Big Top in Battersea Park and undertakes foreign and provincial tours.

Sadler's Wells Royal Ballet tours extensively throughout Britain and also undertakes foreign tours. The company has a London base at Sadler's Wells Theatre.

Information about performances by both companies can be obtained from:
Marketing Department
Royal Opera House
Covent Garden
London WC2E 7QA
Telephone: 01–240 1200
Further information about the companies can be obtained from their respective Press Offices, from the Education Office and from the Archives, all at the Royal Opera House.

London Festival Ballet

The company's main base, in South Kensington, houses the company's studios, archives, and offices for the various departments. The address is:
Festival Ballet House
39 Jay Mews
London SW7 2ES
Telephone: 01–581 1245
London Festival Ballet usually performs at the Royal Festival Hall and the Coliseum in London, and tours throughout the regions and abroad. The publicity department at Festival Ballet House will be pleased to answer enquiries concerning forthcoming performances or publicity material.

For information about the activities and resources offered by the education and community unit, contact the Education and Community Liaison Officer.

Contemporary Dance Trust

London Contemporary Dance Theatre and London Contemporary Dance School are housed at The Place, near St. Pancras and Euston stations. The address is:
The Place
16 Flaxman Terrace
London WC1H 9AT
Telephone: 01–387 0161

Contemporary Dance Theatre offers an Evening School, for adults and teenagers, a Young Place, with week-end classes and workshops for children and teenagers, vacation courses, for all ages and abilities, The Place Theatre, for performances by professional dance companies, by student dancers from the school, and by youth dance groups. The Education and Community Services Department provides teachers, lecture-demonstrations, special events, introductory matinées, residencies, films, booklets, and other material resources for use in schools, colleges and youth organisations.

For information contact the Education and Community Services Officer.

The Scottish Ballet

The company's headquarters are in Glasgow where a specially adapted building houses the dance studios and administrative offices for all aspects of the company's work. The address is:

The Scottish Ballet
261 West Princes Street
Glasgow G4 9EE
Telephone: 041–331 2931

The Scottish Ballet performs at the Theatre Royal in Glasgow and at the King's Theatre in Edinburgh. It also performs at the major theatres in Scotland, Aberdeen, Inverness, Perth and Stirling, as well as making yearly visits to England. Smaller-scale activities are provided throughout Scotland each year where suitable stages exist. For details of performances contact the Publicity and Marketing Officer.

The Scottish Ballet Steps Out group also provide educational and community activities and a dance school associated with the company is in the course of development. Details of this aspect of the work can be obtained from the Director of Young People's and Community Activities.

Glossary of Terms

Arts Council of Great Britain

The Arts Council is an independent body which distributes government money for the arts. Grants are made to professional organisations and individual artists engaged in drama, music and dance, visual arts and literature. The Council also funds Regional Arts Associations, arts centres, community arts; runs exhibitions in London and on tour and also opera, dance and theatre touring.

Ballet Rambert, The Royal Ballet, Sadler's Wells Royal Ballet, London Festival Ballet and London Contemporary Dance Theatre are all partly funded by the Arts Council of Great Britain. Scottish Ballet is partly funded by Scottish Arts Council.

Board of governors/directors/trustees

A group of people who are responsible for the legal and financial aspects of any company and, in the case of a performing company, responsible to their funding bodies for the proper use of public funds. They are not concerned with the day-to-day management of the company.

Ballet master/mistress

The person or people responsible for arranging daily schedules for rehearsals, for taking classes and generally assisting choreographers and producers at rehearsal. In a modern dance company this person is usually called a rehearsal director.

Choreographer

A person who makes dances. A choreographer generally creates dances for many different companies. A choreographer who is based permanently with a specific company for a period of time is called a resident choreographer. A choreographer who has formed a close relationship with a specific company and returns periodically to create dances for them is called an associate choreographer.

Classical ballet

A technique which has evolved over the past 300 years. It was initially based on principles laid down by the early dancing masters such as Pierre Beauchamp and John Weaver, subsequently codified by Carlo Blasis, and has developed over succeeding years. A main feature which distinguishes it from other forms of dance is that the classical style is based on a 90° turn-out from the hip socket. This gives added mobility in the legs and enhances the line in positions such as the *arabesque* and the *attitude*.

Classical dancers

Dancers in a classical ballet company are generally categorised as follows:

Corps de ballet
Dancers who are not soloists and who normally dance together in a large group.

Coryphée
A dancer who is ranked slightly higher than the *corps de ballet* but does not qualify for the status of soloist. Coryphées usually dance in small groups.

Soloist
A rank above coryphée but below that of principal. Soloists perform in small groups but are also given opportunities to dance alone.

Principal
A leading dancer in the company. The leading female dancer is often called a *ballerina* and the leading male dance is sometimes called a *premier danseur*.

Classics

Major nineteenth-century ballets included in the repertoire/repertory of most classical companies, e.g., *Swan Lake, The Nut-cracker, The Sleeping Beauty*.

Contemporary dance

Used with small c and d, contemporary dance refers to those styles of dance which have arisen in the twentieth century and have been used in dance theatre companies. When used with capital letters, i.e., Contemporary Dance, it generally refers to the kind of dance which originates in the Martha Graham style.

Designers

People who are responsible for the stage design, sometimes called the décor, the costumes or the lighting. Often different people are responsible for each of these aspects but they always work together closely with the choreographer to produce a unified theatrical effect on stage.

Director

The person who has the ultimate responsibilty for the existence and smooth running of the company. In some companies this responsibility is shared between an artistic director and an administrative director.

The artistic director is responsible for deciding the artistic policy of the company. This involves such things as which ballets or dances should be included in the repertoire and which choreographers, dancers, designers and producers should be employed.

The administrative director or administrator is responsible for the financial and organisational management of the company. This involves such things as applying for Arts Council Grants and other funds, paying members of the company, arranging tours at home and abroad.

Some companies call people who are responsible for specific areas of work directors. For example, musical director, technical director or rehearsal director.

A musical director is responsible for the orchestra or group of musicians and for rehearsal pianists. Such a person would also work closely with a choreographer giving advice concerning music and the use of musicians.

A technical director or production manager's responsibilities include supervising the making and building of a new production, the organisation of moving whole productions from one theatre to another and the running of each show.

Rehearsal director. See ballet master/mistress.

Greater London Council

An elected local government council formerly the L.C.C. or London County Council. This body grant aids some London-based dance companies.

Impresario

A person who promotes, organises or manages theatrical entertainment.

Notation

The writing down of dances using symbols. Dances may then be reconstructed or reproduced at a later date. Throughout history there have been many systems of notation which have been used to record dances. There are two systems currently widely used in

Britain, these are Benesh Notation and Labanotation. Each system is named after the founder.

Benesh notation was devised by Rudolf Benesh and his wife Joan in 1955. The copyright term for the system is choreology. A person who records dances using the Benesh system of notation is called a choreologist.

Labanotation was devised by Rudolf Laban in 1928. A person who records dances using this system is called a Labanotator.

Pas de deux/duet
A dance for two people.

Première
First performance of a new production.

Producer
The person who leads and co-ordinates a group of specialists who are responsible for creating a ballet or dance. This group of specialists will include the choreographer, designers and musical director.

Régisseur général
The person with overall responsibility for the rehearsal and staging of all productions in a ballet company.

Repertoire/repertory
A collection of dances which a company has ready to perform at a particular period.

Romantic ballet
Ballets which were produced during the period 1830–70 and which reflected the ideals of the Romantic Movement in the arts generally. Writers, painters, musicians, choreographers and dancers of the Romantic Movement produced works designed to show feeling and warmth. Ballets of the period appealed to the emotions. The themes used involved supernatural beings such as Sylphides and Wilis or rustic scenes in exotic lands. Two famous ballets of this period are *La Sylphide* and *Giselle*.

Sponsorship
A private source of funding. For example an individual, a business organisation or a bank might provide money to produce a new dance.

Stage manager
The person who organises the performance from backstage. She/
He is responsible for giving sound and lighting cues and for
making sure everyone is in their proper place.

Trust
An association which is set up to organise the finances of a
company.

Bibliography

Bland, A. (1981) *The Royal Ballet: the first 50 years*. London: Threshold Books.

Bradley, L. (1946) *Sixteen years of Ballet Rambert*. London: Hinrichsen.

Braunsweg, J. (1973) *Braunsweg's ballet scandals*. London: George Allen and Unwin.

Brinson, P. (1972) *Birth of the Royal Ballet* (Libretto for a Ballet for All programme). London.

Brinson, P. and Crisp, C. (1981) *The Pan book of ballet and dance*. London: Pan Books.

Calouste Gulbenkian Foundation (1980) *Dance education and training in Great Britain*. London: Gulbenkian.

Clarke, M. (1955) *The Sadler's Wells Ballet*. London: A. & C. Black.

Clarke, M. (1962) *Dancers of Mercury*. London: A. & C. Black.

Crisp, C., Sainsbury, A. and Williams, P. (eds.) (1981) *Ballet Rambert: 50 years and on*. London: Mercury Trust.

Dixon, J.S. (1981) *Elaine McDonald*. Leeds: Arno.

Dolin, A. (1960) *Autobiography*. London: Oldbourne.

Dolin, A. (1953) *Markova, her life and art*. London: W.H. Allen.

Gillard, D. (1977) *Beryl Grey*. London: W.H. Allen.

Goodwin, N. (1979) *A ballet for Scotland*. Edinburgh: Canongate.

Koegler, H. (1977) *The concise Oxford dictionary of ballet*. London: O.U.P.

Rambert, M. (1972, republ. 1983) *Quicksilver*. London: Macmillan.

Authors

ROBIN ANDERSON is general administrator of The Scottish Ballet. He is founding chairman of the Scottish Council for Dance, chairman of Margaret Morris Movement and member of the boards of The Scottish Theatre Company and the J.D. Fergusson Art Foundation. He is a fellow of the Pharmaceutical Society and a fellow of the Royal Society of Health.

WERDON ANGLIN, a Canadian, graduated from Carleton University in Ottawa. He has worked as a journalist in both Toronto and London, in the public relations department of the Rank Organisation at Pinewood and as a continuity/script writer for ABC and ATV television. In 1963 he joined Ballet for All. When the company closed in 1978 he was appointed education officer of The Royal Opera House. Since 1982 he has been employed in the Department of Research and Community Development at the Laban Centre, London.

JENNY MANN read Philosophy, Politics and Economics at the University of Oxford and Arts Administration at the City University, London. She was Education Liaison Officer for Ballet Rambert from 1980 to 1983. She currently works as manager for Mantis Dance Company as part of the Dance Umbrella Organisation. She is a member of both the Dance Panel of the Greater London Arts Association and the Dance and Mime Projects and Awards Sub-Committee of the Arts Council of Great Britain.

RICHARD MANSFIELD is the Education and Community Services Officer for Contemporary Dance Trust. He is a qualified teacher. Having trained as a dancer at the London Contemporary Dance School, in 1978 he became Co-ordinator of Academic Studies. He has written various articles on contemporary dance and has lectured and taught throughout Great Britain and abroad. As London Contemporary Dance Theatre's education officer he is responsible for the development of the company's special introductory matinées, residencies, lecture-demonstrations, classes and workshops, and London Contemporary Dance Experience, the new education group.

CLAIRE TEVERSON studied Dance at Roehampton Institute of Higher Education. Having qualified as a teacher she was appointed to Sutton High School for Girls where she taught dance and was responsible for dance productions. She has been a member of London Festival Ballet's Advisory Educators Group since its inception and in 1983 became the company's education and community liaison officer.

JOAN W. WHITE lectures in Dance at Roehampton Institute of Higher Education. She is Moderator for the University of London School Examinations Board and for the London Regional Examining Board. She was instrumental in establishing the G.C.E. 'O' and 'A' level Dance and currently chairs the University of London Subject Panel for Dance, and the Joint East Anglian, London Regional and University of London Subject Committee Working Party on Examinations in Dance at 16+. She is a member of both London Festival Ballet and The Royal Ballet's Education Advisory Panels.

Index

Index

DATE DUE

DATE DUE			
NOV 13 '90			